FIND OUT HOW SMART YOU REALLY ARE...

DECIDE HOW SMART YOU REALLY WANT TO BE!

Ready for a work-out? Now you can really exercise your mental muscles with this high-powered selection of the world's finest...

TESTS AND TEASERS

• • •

READER'S DIGEST PAPERBACKS

Informative . . . . . Entertaining . . . . . Essential . . . . .

Berkley, one of America's leading paperback publishers, is proud to present this special series of the best-loved articles, stories and features from America's most trusted magazine. Each is a one-volume library on a popular and important subject. And each is selected, edited and endorsed by the Editors of Reader's Digest themselves! Watch for these others...

THE ART OF LIVING
SECRETS OF THE PAST
"I AM JOE'S BODY"

THE EDITORS OF READER'S DIGEST

TESTS AND TEASERS

A BERKLEY/READER'S DIGEST BOOK
published by
BERKLEY BOOKS, NEW YORK

Cover design by Sam Salant.

TESTS AND TEASERS

A Berkley / Reader's Digest Book / published by arrangement with Reader's Digest Press

PRINTING HISTORY
Berkley/Reader's Digest Edition:
April 1980
Third printing / March 1981

For information address:
Berkley Publishing Corporation,
200 Madison Avenue, New York, New York 10016

ISBN: 0-425-04552-8

A BERKLEY BOOK® TM 757,375
PRINTED IN THE UNITED STATES OF AMERICA

Grateful acknowledgment is made to the following organizations and individuals for permission to reprint material from the following sources:

Liberty Library Corporation for "Twenty Questions," from *Liberty Magazine*, 1941, copyright © 1940 MacFadden Publishing Inc.; Ben O'Dell for "Kangaroo Words," by Ben O'Dell, appearing in *American Magazine* (February '54); Alfred A. Knopf for "How Logical Are You?" from MATHEMATICAL MAGIC SHOW by Martin Gardner. Copyright © 1965, 1967, 1968, 1975, 1976, 1977 by Martin Gardner. Reprinted by permission of Alfred A. Knopf, Inc; Ben O'Dell for "Can You Juggle Letters?" by Ben O'Dell, appearing in *American Magazine* (January '55); Windmill Books Inc./Simon & Schuster Inc. for "CDB!" condensed from the book *CDB!* by William Steig, copyright © 1968 by William Steig, published by Windmill Books Inc./Simon & Schuster Inc; Mrs. Alice Fixx for "Are You A Genius?" appearing as a MENSA quiz. Write MENSA, Dept. RD3, 1701 Third Street, Brooklyn, N.Y. 11223; Mrs. Robert Wagner for "What's Missing?" and "How Well-Lettered Are You?" by Bennett Cerf, condensed from THE SOUND OF LAUGHTER published by Doubleday & Co.; *Redbook* (October '53) for "How Y's Are You?" by Boris Randolph; McGraw-Hill Book Co. for "Can Mice Sing?" by Alan Devoe, copyright © 1951 by Alan Devoe; John E. Gibson for "Are You A Scatterbrain?" by John E. Gibson appearing in *This Week* (March 23 '58) copyright © 1958 by the United Newspapers Magazine Corp.; *Scientific American* (January '64) for "Just Four Fun," by Martin Gardner from MATHEMATICAL GAMES by Martin Gardner. Copyright © January 1964 by *Scientific American* Inc. All rights reserved; John E. Gibson for "What Do You Know About the Sexes?" appearing in *This Week* (March 31 '57 and August 19 '56); *Saturday Evening Post* (June 5 '48) for "Case of the Empty-Handed Musicians," by B.F. Caslon and Bill Bailey copyright © 1948 by the Saturday Evening Post Co.; T.K. Brown III and James Brown Assn. for "Spellbinder," by T.K. Brown III, copyright © 1976 by Esquire Inc. Permission is granted by the author and his agent, James Brown Assn. Inc.; Mrs. Winifred Rice for "Danger: Loaded Questions," appearing in *This Week* (January 22 '56) copyright © 1956 by the United Newspaper Magazine Corp.; *Outdoor Life* (June '51) for "Campfire Quiz," by Andrew G. Ross, copyright © 1952 by Times Mirror Magazines Inc.; *Tulsa Tribune* (May 28 '68) for "Count 'Em Up, Pt. 1," by Roger Devlin; Thomaston, Ga. *Free Press* for "Count 'Em Up, Pt. 2," by Leon Smith; The Atlanta *Constitution* (June 10 '68) for "Count 'Em Up, Pt. 3," by Leon Smith, quoted by Leo Aikman; Ben O'Dell for "Are You A Word Detective?" appearing in *American Magazine* (March '56); *Parade* (1962) for "What Makes You Blush?" by Judith Ellen-Brown, copyright © 1962 by Parade Publishing Inc; Houston *Post* (November 5 '65) for "Sum Fun," by Maxey Brooke, quoted by George Fuermann; *American Magazine* (January '52) for "What's In Your Scrapbook?" by Boris Randolph; *Family Weekly* (March 31, '63) for "True Or False?" by Jerry Klein, copyright ©1963 by Family Weekly Magazine Inc.; *NRTA Journal* (September 10 '74) for "How's Your Musical Geography?" by Nancy and Dan Carlinsky, copyright © 1979 by NRTA Journal; Curtis Brown Ltd. for "You And

TESTS AND TEASERS

Who Is the Engineer?

The following puzzle, known as the Smith-Jones-Robinson classic, is a lively test of reasoning power. It is reported that, in one group of 240 people trying it, only six came up with the solution. But there is no "catch" in it, and the answer has been worked out by many persons in five to ten minutes. *Every fact* is important, and must be considered.

On a train, Smith, Robinson and Jones are the fireman, brakeman and engineer, but NOT respectively. Also aboard the train are three businessmen who have the same names: a Mr. Smith, a Mr. Robinson and a Mr. Jones.

1. Mr. Robinson lives in Detroit.
2. The brakeman lives exactly halfway between Chicago and Detroit.
3. Mr. Jones earns exactly $20,000 per year.
4. The brakeman's nearest neighbor, one of the passengers, earns exactly three times as much as the brakeman.
5. Smith beats the fireman at billiards.
6. The passenger whose name is the same as the brakeman's lives in Chicago.

Twenty Questions 2

Liberty was a popular magazine of a few decades ago. A feature that many readers turned to first was "20 Questions." Here is a selection of queries from that department.

1. The letters in the name "Anzac" stand for what group of words?

2. Is the rainbow ever seen as a complete circle?

3. What bird can outrun a horse and roar like a lion, but cannot fly?

4. What famous landmark in our country moves backward constantly?

5. Is there any difference between flotsam and jetsam?

6. A man had a clock that struck the hours, and also struck once to mark the half hours. He came home one night late. As he opened the door, he heard the clock strike once. Half an hour later, it struck once. Again, a half hour after that, it struck once, and a half hour after that it struck once again. What time was it when he came in?

7. A hunter left camp and walked five miles due south. At that point he shot a bear. He then walked three miles due west, and found he was the same distance from camp as when he shot the bear. What color was the bear?

8. What do the letters S O S, used as the radio distress signal, stand for?

9. Under what circumstances can a pitcher make four or more strike-outs in one inning?

10. How can you keep liquid cooking in a pot from boiling over?

11. What makes Mexican jumping beans jump?

12. What is shivering for?

13. On what parts of his body does a dog perspire?

14. What famous turn-of-the-century boxer fought in the prize ring for 18 years and never had a black eye or a bloody nose?

15. What fighter pulled this gag? Between rounds in his fight with Joe Louis he was in his corner battered and bleeding. His manager said to him: "You're doing fine—he isn't laying a glove on you." "Then," said the fighter, "you'd better keep an eye on the referee because somebody's knocking the stuffing out of me."

16. Can a bird fly backward?

17. What is the will-o'-the-wisp?

18. Who was the first American President to speak over the radio?

19. What is the Caterpillar Club and why is it so called?

20. Why are they called the "high seas?"

Add a Little Something 3

• By inserting the same letter 16 times in appropriate places this jumble of letters will be transformed into a sentence of some sense: VRYVNINGRNSTARNDIGHTNCNTSXCDINGLY-ASILY.

MORRIS MANDEL

• Add the missing vowels to these three well-known proverbs:

BRDNTHHNDSWRTHTWNTHBSH
LKBFRYLP
STTCHNTMSVSNN

Are You Creative? 4

Tests designed to reveal creative ability are still relatively new, but they are already helping corporations search out men and women with a knack for finding imaginative solutions to old and new problems. Psychologist Eugene Raudsepp, co-founder of Princeton Creative Research, Inc., has conducted creativity workshops for some of the largest industries. Here are examples of the tests he has used. To assess your own creativity, try them, then check the answers in the back of the book.

1. Word Hints to Creativity

OBJECT: Think of a fourth word related to all three words listed below.

Cookies   heart   sixteen   _____

The answer is "sweet." Cookies are sweet; sweet is part of the word "sweetheart" and part of the phrase "sweet sixteen."

Now try these words:

1. surprise	line	birthday	_____
2. base	snow	dance	_____
3. rat	blue	cottage	_____
4. nap	bird	call	_____
5. golf	foot	country	_____
6. tiger	news	plate	_____
7. painting	bowl	nail	_____
8. maple	beet	loaf	_____
9. show	oak	plan	_____
10. light	village	golf	_____

2. Your Choice of Responses Shows Creativity

OBJECT: Check the responses that you feel apply to you.

1. Would you rather be considered:
   a____practical?   b____ingenious?

4

2. Does following a schedule:
   a___appeal to you?   b___cramp you?
3. Do you often get behind in your work?
   a___yes   b___no
4. Do hunches come to you just before you go to sleep?
   a___yes   b___no
5. Do you often fret about daily chores?
   a___yes   b___no
6. Do you like to introduce the speaker at a meeting?
   a___yes   b___no
7. Do you sometimes feel anxious about the success of your efforts?
   a___yes   b___no
8. Do you like work in which you must influence others?
   a___yes   b___no
9. Are you fundamentally contented?
   a___yes   ___no
10. Do you spend many evenings with friends?
    a___yes   b___no
11. Do you frequently daydream?
    a___yes   ___no
12. Do you remember the names of people you meet?
    a___yes   ___no

3. Which Traits Describe You?

OBJECT: Check the adjectives that you believe describe you.

determined	worrying
sensitive	versatile
inventive	tolerant
independent	restless
impulsive	reflective
clear-thinking	popular
cheerful	organized
unassuming	moody
enthusiastic	logical
understanding	good-natured
dependable	absentminded
life-of-party	loyal

How Logical Are You? 5

MARTIN GARDNER

Watch out for unexpected or "catch" answers as you take this infuriating quiz.

1. In a certain African village there live 800 women. Three percent of them are wearing one earring. Of the other 97 percent, half are wearing two earrings, half are wearing none. How many earrings all together are being worn by the women?

2. A logician with some time to kill in a small town decided to get a haircut. The town had only two barbers, each with his own shop. The logician glanced into one shop and saw that it was extremely untidy. The barber needed a shave, his clothes were unkempt, his hair was badly cut. The other shop was extremely neat. The barber was freshly shaved and spotlessly dressed, his hair neatly trimmed. The logician returned to the first shop for his haircut. Why?

3. Smith gave a hotel clerk $15 for his cleaning bill. The clerk discovered he had overcharged and sent a bellboy to Smith's room with five $1 bills. The dishonest bellboy gave three to Smith, keeping two for himself. Smith has now paid $12. The bellboy has acquired $2. This accounts for $14. Where is the missing dollar?

4. A secretary types four letters to four people and addresses the four envelopes. If she inserts the letters at random, each in a different envelope, what is the probability that exactly three letters will go into the right envelopes?

5. If nine thousand nine hundred nine dollars is written as $9909, how should twelve thousand twelve hundred twelve dollars be written?

6. A customer in a restaurant found a dead fly in his coffee. He sent the waiter back for a fresh cup. After a sip he shouted, "This is the *same* cup of coffee I had before!" How did he know?

7. "I guarantee," said the pet-shop salesman, "that this parrot will repeat every word it hears." A customer bought the parrot but found it would not speak a single word. Nevertheless, the salesman told the truth. Can you explain?

8. Give at least two ways a barometer can be used to determine the height of a tall building.

Kangaroo Words 6

BEN L. O'DELL

A kangaroo word is one which carries within its spelling (in normal order) a smaller word which is a perfect synonym for itself. For example, note how the word FEASTS contains, in its natural sequence, the synonym, EATS. Listed below are several more of these baby-toting words. So hop to it and see if you can find the synonym hiding in each one.

1. DECEASED
2. ILLUMINATED
3. FABRICATION
4. SALVAGE
5. SEPARATE
6. CATACOMB
7. SATISFIED
8. EXISTS
9. RECLINE
10. APPROPRIATE
11. ROTUND
12. OBSERVE
13. REVOLUTION
14. MARKET
15. FACADE
16. DELIBERATE
17. PANTALOONS
18. PRECIPITATION
19. SUPERVISOR
20. HOSTELRY

Can You Juggle 7 Letters?

BEN L. O'DELL

Turn each pair of radically different words, below, into synonyms by taking a single letter from either word and placing it somewhere within the other one, without rearranging any other letters. As an illustration, by taking the E from RIPE and inserting it into TAR, you get RIP and TEAR.

1. TAR .... RIPE ....

2. DIED .... ANTE ....

3. WHILED .... SPURN ....

4. GROVE .... ROUT ....

5. CURT .... CAVE ....

6. PEST .... CARES ....

7. LICE .... RELINE ....

8. SALVE .... SAVAGE ....

9. SHRED .... BAN ....

10. OUR .... START ....

11. FLAT .... PUMP ....

12. LOPES .... SHILLS ....

CDB! 8

WILLIAM STEIG

I M N N-D-N.

O, I C.

D Y-N S X-L-N !

E S D 1 4 U 2 C.

D L-F-N 8 D A.

H-U !

I M 2 O-L 4 U.

I M C-N A G-P-C.

I M A U-M B-N.
U R N N-M-L.

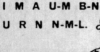

M N X S L-T 4 U !

9

Quote or Misquote?

PETER DONCHIAN

Can you complete these 12 popular quotes *correctly?* Consider three right something of an accomplishment, four an occasion for congratulation, five a minor miracle. To get them all, you need to be a pedant—or peek!

1. Pride goeth before _____
2. To _____ the lily
3. A little _____ is a dangerous thing
4. A penny for your _____
5. Music hath charms to sooth a _____
6. Imitation is the sincerest _____ flattery
7. Ask me no questions, and I'll tell you _____
8. Give him an inch, he'll take _____
9. Variety's the _____ of life
10. _____ is the root of all evil
11. Water, water, everywhere, _____ drop to drink
12. I only regret that I have but _____ for my country

One and Only

F.W. HIGINBOTHAM

The six letters in the word "chesty" can be arranged into only one other word in the English language. What is that word?

Can Mice Sing? 11

ALAN DEVOE

Here's an intriguing quiz to test your knowledge of animals. Answer the questions below, then check your answers with those at the back of the book.

1. Why do animals' eyes shine in the dark?

2. Are bats "as blind as bats"?

3. Why are bulls particularly excited by the color red?

4. Are baby porcupines and similar quilly animals born headfirst so that the mother isn't injured by the quills?

5. Can mice sing?

6. Is it true that an elephant never forgets?

7. Why do we so rarely find dead animals?

8. Do all birds build nests?

9. Why don't sleeping birds fall off their perches?

10. Are snakes slimy?

11. Is it true that snakes can't bite unless they can coil and strike?

12. How can fish jump up big waterfalls?

13. Do fish sleep?

14. Do crocodiles weep crocodile tears?

15. Why don't spiders get snared in their own webs?

16. Can horses sleep standing up?

Are You a Genius? 12

Of course you're smart, but are you brainy enough to qualify for Mensa, the international organization whose only requirement for membership is an I.Q. in the "genius" range? In addition to professors and scientists, the Mensa membership includes belly dancers, farmhands, waitresses, postmen and a number of convicted criminals—which would seem to demonstrate that superior intelligence, while nice to have, does not guarantee success, affluence or even respectability. Take this test to find out if *you* belong among the intellectual elite. Time yourself; there are bonus points for finishing in less than 15, 20 or 25 minutes.

1. Which of the lower boxes best completes the series on the top?

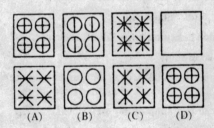

(A)   (B)   (C)   (D)

2. I am a man. If Larry's son is my son's father, what relationship am I to Larry?

(a) His grandfather   (d) His grandson
(b) His father   (e) I am Larry
(c) His son   (f) His uncle

3. Which word does not belong in the following group?

(a) Knife   (c) Smile   (e) Lovely

(b) Swan   (d) Feather   (f) Thought

4. Which two shapes below represent mirror images of the same shape?

(A)   (B)   (C)   (D)   (E)

5. What number comes next in this series?

$$9, 16, 25, 36, \ldots$$

6. Complete this analogy with a five-letter word ending with the letter "H."

High is to low as sky is to ____H.

7. In the box below, a rule of arithmetic applies across and down the box so that two of the numbers in a line produce the third. What is the missing number?

6	2	4
2	?	0
4	0	4

8. Complete this analogy with a seven-letter word ending with the letter "T."

Potential is to actual as future is to _____T.

9. In the group below, find the two words whose meanings do not belong with the others.

(a) glue   (d) nail

(b) sieve   (e) string

(c) buzz saw   (f) paper clip

10. Mountain is to land as whirlpool is to:

(a) forest   (c) sea   (e) shower

(b) wet   (d) sky

11. Find the number that logically completes the series:

$$2, 3, 5, 9, 17, \ldots$$

12. Two of the shapes below represent mirror images of the same shape. Which are they?

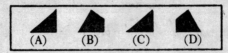

(A)   (B)   (C)   (D)

13. Statistics indicate that men drivers are involved in more accidents than women drivers. The only conclusion that can certainly be drawn is that:

(a) Male chauvinists are wrong, as usual, about women's abilities.
(b) Men are actually better drivers but drive more frequently.
(c) Men and women drive equally well, but men log more total mileage.
(d) Most truck drivers are men.
(e) There is not enough information to justify a conclusion.

14. In the box below, a rule of arithmetic applies across and down the box so that two of the numbers in a line produce the third. What is the missing number?

6	2	12
4	5	20
24	10	?

15. If A × B = 24, C × D = 32, B × D = 48 and B × C = 24, what does A × B × C × D equal?
    (a) 480   (c) 744   (e) 824
    (b) 576   (d) 768

16. Which word does not belong in this group?
(a) microscope   (d) telescope
(b) magnifying glass   (e) telegraph
(c) microphone

17. Find the two words nearest in meaning to each other.
(a) beam   (c) giggle   (e) collection
(b) lump   (d) ray

14

18. Which of the four lower selections best completes the series on the top?

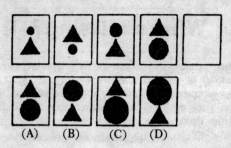

    (A)   (B)   (C)   (D)

19. If Jim turns right *or* left at the stop sign he will run out of gas before he reaches a service station. He has already gone too far past a service station to return before he runs out of gas. He does not see a service station ahead. Only one of the following statements can be positively deduced:

(a) He may run out of gas.

(d) He is lost.

(b) He will run out of gas.

(e) He should turn right at the stop sign.

(c) He should not have taken this route.

(f) He should turn left at the stop sign.

20. Complete the following analogy:

as + – 0 are to:

(a) + – 0   (c) – + 0   (e) + + 0

(b) 0 + –   (d) 0 – +

What's Missing? 13

1. How many times a day do you use the telephone? How often in every month do you dial numbers? Chances are, your answer to the second question ranges into the hundreds. So, without looking at your telephone dial, answer this question: What letters of the alphabet are missing from the dial?

JOYCE BROTHERS AND EDWARD P. F. EAGAN

2. One little poem includes every letter in the alphabet but one. How long will it take you to spot the missing letter?

A jovial swain should not complain
Of any buxom fair,
Who mocks his pain and thinks it gain
To quiz his awkward air.

BENNETT CERF

Oops! 14

Their are three errers in this item. Study it carefully and see if you can find all three of them.

How Y's Are You? 15

BORIS RANDOLPH

The Y and wherefore of the little game below is to add a Y to each word given, wherefore you can arrange the letters to form a new word. For instance: Add a Y to THOU, rearrange, and you get YOUTH. This is a good chance to Y's up on your anagramability.

1. BASS
2. GRIND
3. IDLE
4. DRONE
5. RUBE
6. STORE
7. BEAM
8. TIMES
9. CHAT
10. HONED
11. NEAR
12. PAPER
13. SEAT
14. PALER
15. STAR
16. RELAY
17. DOLE
18. NOMAD
19. ORAL-
20. MAULS

Want to Bet? 16

MARTIN GARDNER

In daily life we constantly make decisions based on our common-sense estimates of probability. Intuition is generally reliable in such matters—but not always. For example:

1. At a party, you find 23 people present. What odds that no two were born on the same day of the same month?

2. A gambling friend offers to bet that, of the license plates on the next 20 passing cars, at least two will match each other in their last two digits. Should you take the bet?

3. Pick two Americans at random—Ms A and Mr. B—and the chances are about 1 in 200,000 they'll know each other. But how likely is it that A will know someone who knows someone who knows B?

4. If a family has three children, what's the likelihood the three will all be of the same sex?

5. If a couple plan to have four children, which is more probable: a) two boys and two girls, or b) three of one sex and one of the other?

6. You flip a coin and it comes up heads 10 times in a row. What odds, then, that it will come up tails on the next flip?

Write Your Own Poem 17

WILL STANTON

There is a land to all men known
Where nothing ever stands alone
Where things are always "something and"
Connected by an ampersand.

Cup & saucer, north & ....
Dun & Bradstreet, hoof & ....
Rough & ready, curds & ....
Bag & baggage, Bob & ....
Off & running, neck & ....
Black & Decker, hunt & ....
Cloak & dagger, bill & ....
Fair & warmer, me & ....
High & mighty, push & ....
Lea & Perrins, cock & ....
One & only, pick & ....
Horse & buggy, P's & ....
Come & get it, touch & ....
Up & at 'em, yes & ....
Toil & trouble, ways & ....
Tar & feathers, pork & ....
Bread & butter, love & ....
Drunk & disorderly, Mr. & ....
Trial & error, heaven & ....
Death & taxes, hail & ....

19

Are You a Scatterbrain? 18

JOHN E. GIBSON

One of the most ingenious tests for self-analysis is the Proverbs Test developed by Prof. Donald R. Gorham of Baylor University. Used professionally, it measures emotional attitudes and vocational aptitudes, and is a key to personality traits. With it Professor Gorham found he could spot types such as the practical person, the scatterbrain, the deeply moral person.

The complete test includes 40 proverbs. For each proverb in this shorter version, check off the interpretation that seems most logical. Keep in mind, this is not a test in which you are right or wrong: it is designed to reveal only what the proverbs mean to you.

1. A tree is known by the fruit it bears.
   a. Only a fool would look for apples in a pear tree.
   b. As the twig is bent, the tree will lean.
   c. A man is known by his deeds.
   d. Evil can never be disguised.

2. Don't cross bridges until you get to them.
   w. Don't burn your bridges ahead of you.
   x. Heaven helps a man who has faith in the future.
   y. Do today's job right; don't keep fussing about tomorrow's.
   z. Don't worry about troubles till they come.

3. The harder the storm, the sooner it's over.
   a. The worst thunderstorms don't last long.
   b. It's calmest after a storm.
   c. Our large problems are often solved more quickly than our small ones.
   d. The harder one works, the softer one's bed.

4. He thinks not well that thinks not again.

w. Your second thought is better than your first.
x. Only the Lord loves a blunderer and even He finds it trying.
y. Always double-check your work for errors.
z. The good plan is the thoroughly considered plan.

5. Set a thief to catch a thief.

a. Because a thief knows where thieves hang out.
b. It is all right to employ a criminal if he can help justice.
c. If you have a special problem, consult someone who has special knowledge about it.
d. Evil must be its own downfall.

6. Beauty is only skin-deep.

w. All women are sisters under the skin.
x. A woman may paint her face but not her soul.
y. Pretty packages don't make good merchandise.
z. Character is more important than outward appearance.

7. Too much water drowns the miller.

a. Never build on uncertain ground.
b. You'll never get wet if you don't go near the water.
c. Even good things can be overdone.
d. Riches and ruin both start with an *r*.

8. The thread breaks where it is weakest.

w. A stitch in time saves nine.
x. A good man is not just 99 percent good.
y. One poor bit of workmanship can ruin a whole job.
z. A flaw in one's character will show up under pressure.

9. He who rides the tiger cannot dismount.

a. Don't tackle anything you can't finish.
b. A tiger can't change his stripes.
c. A risky venture is often hard to get free of.
d. One moment of folly can mean a lifetime of regret.

10. A change of pasture makes fat calves.

w. The grass is always greener in the other fellow's yard.
x. Charity begins at home but never stops there.
y. You can't eat the same bread twice.
z. New experiences stimulate people.

What Do You Know About the Sexes? 19

JOHN GIBSON

How much do you really know about the sexes? See how your true-or-false answers to these simple questions about men and women agree with the findings of psychologists and sociologists.

1. Husband-wife arguments are usually won by the spouse who does the most talking.　　T—　F—
2. Women are better at solving complicated problems than men.　　T—　F—
3. Women tend to be more cheerful and optimistic than men.　　T—　F—
4. Men get along on less sleep than women.　　T—　F—
5. When faced with a severe crisis, a woman is more likely to go to pieces than a man.　　T—　F—
6. Men are fussier about their food.　　T—　F—
7. Men tend to be more self-centered than women.　　T—　F—
8. When a couple has mother-in-law trouble, it's usually the wife's mother who is to blame.　　T—　F—
9. Women talk more about men than men talk about women.　　T—　F—
10. Wives understand their husbands better than their husbands understand them.　　T—　F—
11. Women make more fuss about minor and non-existent ailments.　　T—　F—
12. Men are more truthful than women.　　T—　F—

13. Most husbands are more intelligent than their wives. T— F—
14. Divorced men are better second marriage risks than divorced women. T— F—
15. The widespread masculine belief that women are the most talkative sex actually has no basis in fact. T— F—
16. Women are more easily bored than men. T— F—
17. Men have quicker reflexes, react faster than women. T— F—
18. Men have a greater capacity for happiness than women. T— F—

Just Four Fun 20

MARTIN GARDNER

See how many whole numbers you can form, starting with 1 and going through 10, by using only the digit 4 four times—no more, no less—and the multiplication, division, addition and/or subtraction signs.

Samples: 1 = 44/44   2 = 4/4 + 4/4

By adding the square-root sign, 11 through 18 are readily obtainable. So start with 3 and see how far you can go.

Case of the Empty-Handed Musicians

B. F. CASLON AND BILL BAILEY

The musicians sketched here are working under one bad handicap—they haven't got their usual instruments. Nevertheless, you ought to be able to tell from the positions they're in what instrument each plays. The gent clawing the air in Picture Number 1 obviously is a piano player without his piano; maybe it's better that way. What do the others play? You should be able to equip six out of nine.

Spellbinder 22

T. K. BROWN III

A test of 60 common but hard-to-spell English words was given to 800 college graduates— among them a high proportion of teachers, editors, journalists, proofreaders, advertising men and women. *Not a single one* of these linguistically sophisticated people got a perfect score. The 20 words they missed most often are listed below, grotesquely misspelled. Try your luck?

1. Ass'-uh-9
2. brag-uh-doe'-C-O
3. rare'-uff-I
4. lick'-wuff-I
5. puh-vill'-yun
6. ver-mill'-yun
7. im-pah'-stir
8. mock'-uh-sun
9. uh-kahm'-uh-date
10. kon-sen'-sus
11. roe-ko'-ko
12. tit'-tle-8
13. sack-ruh-li'-jus
14. may'-uh-naze
15. im-pray-sor'-ry-O
16. in-ock'-U-late
17. soo'-per-seed
18. obly-gah'-to
19. des'-suh-Kate
20. re-sus'-suh-tate

Danger: Loaded Questions 23

CHARLES D. RICE

These questions seem easy, but think twice before answering, because they're tricky.

1. Adam and Eve were banished from the Garden of Eden for eating what fruit?

2. Who said, "Everybody talks about the weather but nobody does anything about it"?

3. In what year was Christ born?

4. How much more reflected light do we get from a full moon than from a half-moon: Twice as much? The same amount? Four times as much? Seven times as much?

5. Boris Karloff gained his greatest success playing a weird character in the movies. Who was the character?

6. Which of the following rid Ireland of snakes? a) The Royal Zoological Society. b) Nobody—there were never any snakes there. c) Irish terriers. d) St. Patrick.

7. What was the highest title that Julius Caesar acquired: king, emperor, dictator or consul?

8. Where was the Battle of Bunker Hill fought?

9. Was Charles Lindbergh the first person to cross the Atlantic Ocean by air? Or the third, fifth, fourteenth, or what?

Campfire Quiz 24

ANDREW G. ROSS

1. You wake up in a pitch-black room in a hunting lodge, and there's no light handy. In your duffel bag there are six black socks and six white ones, all mixed together. You want to pick out a matching pair. What is the smallest number of socks you can take out of the bag and be sure of getting a pair of the same color?

2. A bass plug and some touch-up paint cost a total of $2.50. The plug costs $2 more than the paint. What is the cost of each?

3. A deep-sea fishing boat is lying in the harbor. Over its side hangs a rope ladder, with its end just touching the water. Rungs of the ladder are one foot apart. The tide rises at the rate of eight inches an hour. At the end of six hours how many of the rungs will be covered?

4. How much dirt is there in a hole 1 ft. by 1 ft. by 1 ft.?

5. A camp cook wanted to measure four ounces of syrup out of a jug but he had only a five-oz. and a three-oz. bottle. How did he manage it?

Are You a Word Detective? 25

BEN L. O'DELL

Your ability as a word sleuth is put to the test in this game. On each line below are three clues to a familiar word: a rhyme for the word; what it means spelled backward; and a word with which it makes a phrase. For example, a word answering all three hints in No. 1 would be STAR.

It rhymes with	Spelled backward, it means	It makes a phrase with	Answer
1. Char	Tattles (slang)	Shooting	STAR
2. Reap	Strips off skin	Tight	_____
3. Shrug	Swallow hard	Spark	_____
4. Gnaw	Skin blemishes	Last	_____
5. Sieve	Moral wrong	High	_____
6. Sons	Comfortable; cozy	Great	_____
7. Leap	Look at furtively	House	_____
8. Chart	Capture; snare	Company	_____
9. Flag	Slang for revolvers	Party	_____
10. Fog	A sailor	Down	_____
11. Bored	Pull; haul	Boss	_____
12. Revel	Existed	Poor	_____

Count 'Em Up 26

Eight men are in a room. Each man shakes hands with each of the others once. How many handshakes are there?

ROGER DEVLIN

Be prepared for the answer by the time you finish reading this paragraph, without retracing your steps: A bus started out empty. At the first stop it picked up 10 passengers. Stopping again, it let off five passengers and picked up 12. At the next stop, eight passengers got on and two got off. When the bus stopped again, 14 passengers got on and nine got off. One more stop and two passengers got on and one got off.

Ready with your answer?

The question: How many stops did the bus make?

LEON SMITH

What Makes You Blush? 27

JUDITH-ELLEN BROWN

Why do you blush? Is it modesty? Guilt feelings? Or does the color rise because you hate to be the center of attention? Dr. Sandor S. Feldman, clinical professor of psychiatry at the University of Rochester School of Medicine and Dentistry, studied the subject for many years and became perhaps the world's foremost authority in this field. In the quiz below, check your answers against his.

1. People blush only when with others, never when alone. True False
2. A baby can't blush. True False
3. Women blush more than men. True False
4. Only people of light-skinned races blush. True False
5. As you grow older, you're less likely to blush. True False
6. Women don't blush as much as their grandmothers did. True False
7. You blush only at your own acts. True False
8. Blushing can be contagious. True False
9. When you blush, only your face gets red. True False
10. Blushing can be controlled by conscious effort. True False

What's in Your Scrapbook? 28

BORIS RANDOLPH

Each item defined below can be spelled from letters contained in the word SCRAPBOOK. You may use a letter in any word only as often as it occurs in SCRAPBOOK. Ten correct is passing; 15 or more right, excellent.

1. Small stocking ....
2. Playground ....
3. Thief ....
4. Shellfish ....
5. Wild pig ....
6. Chef ....
7. Tree ....
8. Ghost ....
9. Snake ....
10. Another snake ....
11. Still another snake ....
12. Policeman ....
13. Boulder ....
14. Bag ....
15. Stream ....
16. Country bumpkin ....
17. Shovel ....
18. Crowlike bird ....
19. Automobile ....
20. Barrel ....

True or False? 29

JERRY KLEIN

To avoid the dunce cap, you'll have to identify correctly as true or false at least half the following statements. The answers may seem obvious—but watch out!

1. Cleopatra was a pure-blooded Egyptian princess.

2. Frankenstein was the name of a fictional monster created by a mad doctor.

3. The 21st century will start on January 1 in the year 2000.

4. Wherever you may be, you need only locate the North Star to find your direction.

5. Cream is heavier than milk.

6. It is illegal to deface coins.

7. In 1927 Charles A. Lindbergh made the first nonstop flight across the Atlantic Ocean.

8. The liner *Lusitania* was torpedoed in 1915 on her maiden voyage.

9. The kilt originated in Scotland.

10. The republican form of government originated in ancient Greece.

11. The porcupine shoots its quills to fight off enemies.

12. Diamonds will not burn.

13. A pound of feathers and a pound of gold are the same weight.

33

How's Your Musical Geography? 30

NANCY AND DAN CARLINSKY

You may know more about the world's cities, states, countries—and even some streets—than you imagine. To take this spot quiz, match each sentence with the appropriate location from the list on the following page. Twenty correct answers is good; over 30 means you really know the score, geographically.

AMERICAN STATES

1) Where the cotton and the corn and 'taters grow. 2) There's a waltz named after this state (and it's not Missouri). 3) And a polka named after this one. 4) It's best to be here in the morning. 5) Where bowers of flowers bloom in the sun. 6) Rodgers and Hammerstein collaborated on this musical. 7) In "Oh, Susanna," the singer with the banjo on his knee hails from here. 8) Home of the Yellow Rose. 9) A very popular girl knocked 'em dead in the 1920s; this state named and claimed her.

AMERICAN CITIES

10) There's a pawnshop on the corner here. 11) Referred to as the land of dreamy scenes, it has Creole babies with flashing eyes. 12) Tony Bennett left his heart here. 13) Where Mamie O'Rorke tripped the light fantastic. 14) A famous shoeshine boy worked here. 15) Referred to as Big D. 16) A woman promised to dance the hoochee-koochee with her husband at a fair in this town. 17) To Oklahomans, this place had all the features of the "modern" world: gas buggies, skyscrapers seven stories high and inside privies. 18) In this town you might see a man dancing with his wife.

FOREIGN AFFAIRS

19) Where to go by slow boat. 20) They're askin' how 'tis back in the old hometown. 21) Precipitation here usually occurs in the flatlands. 22) Where the walls came tumbling down. 23) Mozart's Symphony No. 38 in D is popularly called by the name of this European capital. 24) In summer, this place sizzles. In winter, it drizzles. 25) The high road and the low road both lead to this country. 26) French children sing of this town's famous bridge that folks dance on. 27) The everlasting light shines in the dark streets of this little town.

HERE AND THERE

28) After you give my regards to old Broadway, remember me to _____. 29) A singer lost a lover here by courting too slow. 30) This place should be remembered, along with the girl that has loved you so true. 31) Old times here are not forgotten. 32) An old ballad calls this a rolling river. 33) This San Francisco street looks down from Chinatown. 34) In the movie, *Go Into Your Dance*, Al Jolson is introduced to a Spanish-style dancer. She's not from Madrid or Havana, she's from _____. 35) Ruby Keeler did a tap dance on top of a taxicab here. 36) Where the grain is amber, and the mountains are purple.

Alabama	Georgia	Pennsylvania
America	Glocca Morra	Pittsburgh
Avignon	Grant Avenue	Prague
Bethlehem	Herald Square	Red River Valley
California	Jericho	St. Louis
Carolina	Kansas City	San Francisco
Chattanooga	Manhattan	Scotland
Chicago	New Orleans	Shenandoah
China	New York	Spain
Dallas	Oklahoma	Tennessee
Dixie	Old Smoky	Texas
42nd Street	Paris	Virginia

You and the Weather 31

HAROLD B. CHURCHILL

Most of us have our own ideas about how weather and climate affect our everyday life—some right, some weirdly wrong. Here's a chance to check your ideas against those of medical climatologists. Answer true or false.

1. Summer is an ideal time for a vacation. T— F—
2. Your baby's weight is influenced by the month in which he's conceived. T— F—
3. We're all more irritable before a storm. T— F—
4. We're more efficient in cold weather than warm. T— F—
5. Mild winters are not healthy. T— F—
6. Girls mature earlier in a tropical climate. T— F—
7. Spring fever is imaginary. T— F—
8. Marital quarrels hit their peak in July. T— F—
9. Babies wet more in wet weather. T— F—
10. Children are more unruly when the weather is dry. T— F—
11. June, the month of romance and marriage, is also a peak month for insanity, homicide and crime. T— F—
12. Thin people are more sensitive to the weather. T— F—
13. We all work better in good weather. T— F—
14. Storms are stimulating. T— F—

Vowel Play 32

1. There is at least one English word in which a single vowel is repeated six times. What's the word?

ROGER DEVLIN

2. Can you think of at least three words of five letters or more, none of which contains the letters A, E, I, O or U?

ROGER DEVLIN

3. How far do you have to count before using the letter A in spelling a number?

CEDRIC ADAMS

The Great Chain Puzzle 33

If it costs five cents to break a link, and ten cents to weld it again—what is the least it would cost to join in a single length of chain the five segments shown here?

Sixty cents? Try again—the correct answer is less.

There's a simple moral to this: The obvious way is not always the most economical way.

Quiz-Show Questions 34

The electronic media discovered long ago that it takes something special to beat the challenge of an interesting interrogatory. Here is a selection of questions that were asked and answered on the air in the popular radio quiz programs of the 1940s.

1. How does one know which is the left bank and which is the right bank of a river?

2. What popular dances had in their titles the name of (1) a pastry, (2) a fruit, (3) a city?

3. Is a person who is excessively thirsty suffering from kleptomania, polydipsia, or myopia?

4. True or false? Noah's Ark was known as the Ark of the Covenant.

5. In a deck of ordinary playing cards, two of the Jacks are one-eyed; the other Jacks have two eyes. What is the total number of eyes on the four Jack cards?

6. Is it true that there is one place in England where the King or Queen can never go?

7. If you are convicted of the crime of embracery, what have you done?

8. Of what well-known proverb is this a paraphrase? "A nomadic portion of the metamorphosed igneous or sedimentary deposits of the Proterozoic era accumulates no bryophytic plant life."

9. Why would a detective doubt this story? A lady, dreaming that she was drowning, became so frightened that she died of a heart attack in her sleep.

10. Most of us use it every day in our homes. If we purchased 100 pounds of it, it would contain approximately 87 pounds of water; 4 pounds of fat; 4 pounds of casein, ash and albumin; and 5 pounds of sugar. What is it?

11. Five automobiles were lined up bumper-to-bumper. How many bumpers were actually touching each other?

12. Why does it take longer to hoist a flag to half-mast than it does to hoist it to full-mast?

13. If an elderly man is the scion of a prominent family, is he the founder of the family; a descendant of the family; or the black sheep of the family?

14. Niagara Falls is situated between which two of the Great Lakes?

15. If you were a musician and were practicing your flams, your flam paradiddles, your double paradiddles, ruffs, and double drags, what kind of musical instrument would you be playing?

16. Is the toe of Italy's boot on the west or east side of the peninsula?

17. How many keys has a piano—66, 77, 88, or 99?

18. Mr. and Mrs. Smith had seven daughters and each daughter had one brother. How many people were in the Smith family?

19. You've heard the threat, "I'll break every bone in your body." In order to do it, how many bones would you have to break: approximately 200, 2000, or 20,000?

20. Would it be cheaper for you to take one friend to the movies twice—or two friends at the same time?

21. There are 14 punctuation marks in English grammar. Can you name eight?

22. Is the tip of the finger, the end of the tongue or the bottom of the feet the most delicate organ of touch?

23. If your doctor gave you three pills and told you to take one every half hour, how long would they last?

24. Name seven articles, each starting with the letter *s*, worn on the feet.

25. What fruit has its seeds on the outside?

26. In baseball, the batter hits a grounder and runs to first base. The shortstop fields the grounder and throws to first, the ball arriving at the same instant as the runner. Is the runner out or safe?

27. Zinc, copper, pewter, bronze, brass—which of these are not alloys?

28. Is a pundit a short pun, a learned man, or one who habitually makes puns?

29. What is the most popular prepared drink in the world?

30. Is a zebra black and white stripes, or white with black stripes?

31. If you entered a dark room and had only one match and there was a kerosene lamp, an oil stove, and a cigarette, which would you light first?

Sum Fun

MAXEY BROOKE

Which would you estimate to be the greater sum, that of the figures on the left, or that of the figures on the right?

987654321	123456789
87654321	12345678
7654321	1234567
654321	123456
54321	12345
4321	1234
321	123
21	12
1	1

Bewitched, Bothered or Befuddled? 36

MARTIN GARDNER

Bronx vs. Brooklyn

A young man lives in Manhattan near a subway express station. He has two girl friends, one in Brooklyn, one in the Bronx. To visit the girl in Brooklyn, he takes a train on the downtown side of the platform; to visit the girl in the Bronx, he takes a train on the uptown side of the same platform. Since he likes both girls equally well, he simply takes the first train that comes along. In this way he lets chance determine whether he rides to the Bronx or to Brooklyn. The young man reaches the subway platform at a random moment each Saturday afternoon. Brooklyn and Bronx trains arrive equally often—every ten minutes. Yet, for some obscure reason, he finds himself spending most of his time with the girl in Brooklyn: in fact, on the average, he goes there nine times out of ten. Can you think of a good reason why the odds so heavily favor Brooklyn?

The Fork in the Road

A logician vacationing in the South Seas finds himself on an island inhabited by the two proverbial tribes of liars and truth-tellers. Members of one tribe always tell the truth; members of the other aways lie. He comes to a fork in the road and has to ask a native bystander which branch he should take to reach a village. He has no way of telling whether the native is a truth-teller or a liar. The logician thinks a moment, then asks *one* question only.

From the reply he knows which road to take. What question does he ask?

Scrambled Box Tops

Three boxes—one containing two black marbles, one containing two white marbles, the third containing one black marble and one white marble—are put before you. The boxes are labeled to indicate their contents—BB, WW and BW—but you are told that the tops have been switched so that every box is now incorrectly labeled. You are asked to take one marble at a time out of any box, without looking inside, and, using this sampling process, to determine the contents of all three boxes. What is the smallest number of drawings you will need to determine the contents of each box?

The Counterfeit Coins

You have ten stacks of coins, each consisting of ten half-dollars. One entire stack is counterfeit, but you do not know which stack it is. You do know the weight of a genuine half-dollar, and you are also told that each counterfeit coin weighs one gram more than the genuine model. You may weigh the coins on a scale. What is the smallest number of weighings necessary to determine which stack is counterfeit?

What's Your Wife's Name? 37

1. Write down the number corresponding to the month of your birth from Table 1.

2. Add the number corresponding to your favorite dish from Table 2.

3. Multiply the answer by ten. Then add three if you want to know the name of your future wife, two for your present wife, one for your last wife.

4. Reverse the order of the figures, and subtract the result from the number you had before reversing. (Thus, 521 becomes 125 on reversing, which is subtracted from 521—leaving 396.)

5. Reverse this answer and add the result to the number it was before reversing.

6. Add 52,205,197 if you are a British Lord; otherwise, add 423,571.

7. Look up the number corresponding to the first letter of your surname in Table 3, and place it on the right-hand side of the previous answer. If, for example, your name is Smith, and the previous answer was 123,456, you would place the two figures corresponding to S, which are 60, on the right, giving you 12,345,660.

8. Repeat this with the next letter of your surname, and continue for all the letters, in order, in your surname.

9. Halve the answer.

10. Divide the answer into groups of two figures. Each group represents a letter of your wife's name, when referred to Table 4. Thus, if the answer is 21-10-23-43, her name will be Mary.

TABLE 1

January	90	July	70
February	80	August	80
March	70	September	90
April	60	October	80
May	50	November	70
June	60	December	60

TABLE 2

Steak and Onions	8
Hamburger and French Fries	7
Ham and Eggs	6
Chicken and Rice	5
Franks and Beans	4
Tuna Fish Casserole	3
Roast Beef and Potatoes	9

TABLE 3

		M – 42	T – 44
A – 20	G – 64	N – 66	U – 28
B – 40	H – 68	O – 26	V – 84
C – 48	I – 24	P – 82	W – 88
D – 62	J – 80	Q – 90	X – 58
E – 22	K – 54	R – 46	Y – 86
F – 50	L – 52	S – 60	Z – 56

TABLE 4

		27 – K	34 – H
10 – A	21 – M	28 – Z	40 – J
11 – E	22 – T	29 – X	41 – P
12 – I	23 – R	30 – S	42 – V
13 – O	24 – C	31 – D	43 – Y
14 – U	25 – F	32 – G	44 – W
20 – B	26 – L	33 – N	45 – Q

45

What Do You Know About Eating? 38

JUDITH CHASE CHURCHILL

Check your knowledge against that of food experts by answering true or false.

1. Breakfast is your most important meal.   T—   F—
2. Hot meals warm you.   T—   F—
3. You should eat less in hot weather.   T—   F—
4. Some foods are sex stimulants.   T—   F—
5. We'd be better off if we ate five times daily.   T—   F—
6. The more you eat the more you want.   T—   F—
7. Exercise is a more efficient way to reduce than diet.   T—   F—
8. Your disposition is worst just before meals.   T—   F—
9. It's almost impossible to overstuff a boy.   T—   F—
10. Food is a good cure for fatigue.   T—   F—
11. If most fat people ate what they say they eat they'd be thin.   T—   F—
12. Bedtime snacks cause restless sleep.   T—   F—

How Well-Lettered Are You? 39

1. Can you name ten parts of the human body (no slang words) that have only three letters?

MICKEY PORTER

2. Give a single letter which expresses each of the following— and if you're right you'll be the first to know it: 1) Blue and white bird. 2) Lowest note on the piano. 3) A large body of water. 4) A girl's nickname. 5) A vegetable. 6) An exclamation. 7) A beverage.

BENNETT CERF

Break the Code 40

The letters, O, T, T, F, F, __, __ form the beginning of an intelligible series. The problem is to add two more letters in the series. Once the problem is solved, an infinite number of letters can be added.

EDWIN DIAMOND

What's Your Maturity Quotient?

LOUIS BINSTOCK

Maturity is a *becoming*—a changing, a progression toward something better. To measure your Maturity Quotient, answer a frank Yes or No to the following 50 questions. Then let your M.Q. score and your response to each question, carefully considered, serve as a lever to pry you loose from immaturities of thought and behavior.

CATEGORY A	Yes	No
1. Do you often say: "I can't cut down on eating"?	☐	☐
2. Do you often give the excuse: "I'm too busy"?	☐	☐
3. Do you often apologize: "I have such a poor memory"?	☐	☐
4. Do you frequently say: "I'm just not sociable"?	☐	☐
5. Do you use the excuse: "If only I had more time"?	☐	☐
6. Do you assert positively: "I'll never do it"?	☐	☐
7. Do you usually wait for someone else to introduce himself first?	☐	☐
8. Do you self-righteously proclaim: "I can't be a hypocrite"?	☐	☐
9. Do you confidently proclaim: "I'm not interested in money"?	☐	☐
10. Do you feel that you can always do things better than anyone else?	☐	☐

CATEGORY B	Yes	No
1. Do you often say: "I intended to do it"?	☐	☐
2. Are you a compulsive talker?	☐	☐
3. Do you excuse yourself with: "I just can't help it"?	☐	☐
4. Do you frequently apologize with: "I'm too tired"?	☐	☐
5. Do you shy away with: "I just can't speak in public"?	☐	☐
6. Do you often say: "I'm sorry, I can't handle money"?	☐	☐
7. Do you judge others on the basis of rumors?	☐	☐
8. Must you be constantly entertained?	☐	☐
9. Must you usually be the center of attraction?	☐	☐
10. Are you resentful when someone doesn't remember you?	☐	☐

CATEGORY C	Yes	No
1. Do you often stop a discussion with: "I know what I'm talking about"?	☐	☐
2. Do you consistently try to tell other people what to do?	☐	☐
3. Do you think that material gifts can create strong friendships?	☐	☐
4. If you don't like a person, do you refuse to deal with him?	☐	☐
5. Is it hard for you to admit you are wrong?	☐	☐
6. Is it difficult for you to apologize?	☐	☐
7. Do you get angry quickly?	☐	☐
8. Do you often say: "People are not friendly"?	☐	☐
9. Do you say to yourself: "If only I had married someone else"?	☐	☐
10. Must you always have the last word?	☐	☐

CATEGORY D	Yes	No
1. Do you expect everyone to love you?	☐	☐
2. Do you expect never to be rebuffed or rejected?	☐	☐
3. Do you assert: "I don't need anyone's help"?	☐	☐
4. Do you frequently say: "It was my idea"?	☐	☐
5. Do you find it hard to take criticism?	☐	☐
6. Do you frequently get into arguments?	☐	☐
7. Are you easily hurt?	☐	☐
8. Do you always expect gratitude?	☐	☐
9. Do you excuse yourself with: "If only I had had his opportunities"?	☐	☐
10. Is it difficult for you to take advice gracefully?	☐	☐

CATEGORY E	Yes	No
1. Must you have everything you want?	☐	☐
2. Do you worry because you worry?	☐	☐
3. Do you brood over disappointments?	☐	☐
4. Do you feed on grudges?	☐	☐
5. Have you a drive for perfection?	☐	☐
6. Must you always be happy?	☐	☐
7. Must you always have your way?	☐	☐
8. Does someone else's success trouble you?	☐	☐
9. Do you hesitate to sacrifice for a meaningful objective?	☐	☐
10. Is it difficult for you to trust anyone?	☐	☐

Arithmetics 42

1. From Jerome S. Meyer's book *Fun With Mathematics*, "Make 1000 by using only eight 8's."

BERT BACHARACH

2. Here's a little drill in mental arithmetic to sharpen your skills. Do this in your head:

> Add one thousand twenty and one thousand twenty.... Now add twenty to your answer.... Add twenty again.... Now add ten.... And add ten again. What's your total?

RAY ORROCK

3. This one has been used by some personnel directors in oral aptitude tests. You're supposed to answer it in one and a half minutes:

> If a man-and-a-half can eat a pie-and-a-half in a minute-and-a-half, how many men would it take to eat 60 pies in 30 minutes?

4. Bored and restless? Try writing your zip code in Roman numerals.

JACKIE VERNON

5. A chemist discovered that a certain chemical reaction took 80 minutes when he wore a wool jacket. But when he wasn't wearing the jacket, the same reaction always took an hour and 20 minutes. Can you explain?

Four-Minute Challenges

JULES LEOPOLD

Sooner or later, someone is sure to challenge you to try one of these familiar but tantalizing after-dinner problems. Why not get in some preprandial practice? Allow yourself no more than four minutes for each challenge.

1. Pop-Off. Place a dollar bill flat on a table. Turn an empty pop bottle upside down so that its mouth rests on the center of the bill. Without tipping over the bottle, and allowing nothing to touch the bottle other than the bill or the table, remove the dollar bill from beneath the bottle.

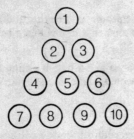

2. Reversal. A triangle of ten pennies points away from you. Moving only three pennies, make the triangle point toward you.

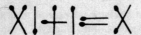

3. Runaround. Arrange ten matches so that they create the equation in Roman numbers: XI + I = X. This equation is, of course, incorrect. Make the equation read correctly without touching anything.

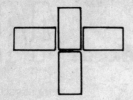

4. Foursquare. Place four rectangular cards of identical size in the positions shown. Now form a square by moving only one card.

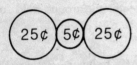

5. Shift. Set a nickel between two quarters with its edges touching both. Now get the right-hand quarter into the middle position without moving the nickel or touching the left-hand quarter.

6. Two-by-Four. Twelve matches are placed to form four squares. Remove two matches and leave only two squares.

7. Tip-Off. "Here's how we'll settle who tips the waiter," says a friend at lunch. He tears one paper match out of a matchfolder. "I'll toss it. If it lands on either side, I'll pay. If it stands on edge, you pay." Should you agree?

What One Word?

BEN L. O'DELL

Can you find the single word which will be a *synonym* for *both* the words in each pair that follows? For example, the word that would be a common synonym to *Sort* and *Benevolent* is *Kind*. You should be able to supply 12 double-duty-words for the remaining groups, but 15 or more is excellent.

1. Sort—Benevolent
2. Results—Belongings
3. Curtsy—Prow
4. Stays—Corpse
5. Railing—Duel
6. Tresses—Fastens
7. Dissertation—Try
8. Ray—Timber
9. Intersect—Peevish
10. Raise—Back
11. Eruption—Reckless
12. Calculate—Shape
13. Hoodwink—Cliff
14. Tied—Leap
15. Wearied—Drilled
16. Scrape—Grille
17. Ravine—Stuff
18. Stockings—Tube
19. Spiritualist—Average
20. Cataract—Drops

The Triangle Game

RALPH A. BROOK

If past experience holds true, the odds are 40 to 1 you can't read correctly the simple phrases in the triangles below. Look at each one in turn, and repeat aloud—or write down—what you think it says, before checking the answers in the back of the book.

Try This for Fun 46

GORDON GAMMACK

Without stopping to think or plan, name—just as they pop into mind—a color, any number from one to ten, a flower, a fruit.

Compare your answers with the ones most people give, as noted in the back of the book.

"Information Please"

One of the most popular radio program series ever produced was the famous "Information Please" in which a panel of experts answered questions from radio listeners. Here is a group of typical questions submitted by the public in an attempt to "stump the experts."

1. Two groups of campers, one on the seacoast and one on a high mountain, drop eggs into boiling water. Which campers will get hard-boiled eggs first?

2. Give the origin of each of the following words: bloomers, sandwich, guillotine, Vandyke, gerrymander.

3. Name the athletic games in which the following number of contestants constitute a team: 2, 4, 6, 8, 10.

4. What are our equivalents of these British terms: petrol; multiple shops; road diversion; hire-purchase system; butter muslin?

5. Why would it never be necessary for the man in the moon, if married to a chatterbox, to tell her to shut up?

6. What European Premier was saved from execution because he was an American citizen?

7. Give five musical terms which can also be applied to baseball.

8. Does an Arab prefer white horses to black horses because they run faster, withstand the sun better, eat less or are more beautiful?

9. Where is the Island of Reil?

10. Who was Shakespeare's favorite actress?

11. Distinguish between: Mazuma; Mazola; Montezuma; Zeugma; Sigma.

12. Which of the following will see more clearly in total darkness? Owl; Bat; Leopard.

13. Is it possible for an airplane to go backwards?

The Match Maneuver

SAMM S. BAKER

The challenge is to position six ordinary wooden kitchen matches so that each one touches every other one firmly. This may be tougher than you think. If you try to arrange the matches like the spokes of a wheel, bringing the heads or ends together at the center, their thickness prevents the solution.

How Persuasive Are You? 49

JOHN H. WOLFE

Practically every day, each of us faces at least one situation in which we must try to persuade someone to do what we want. Here are ten fairly typical situations. What would you choose in each instance as the likeliest approach to resolve the problem?

1. **You're trying to persuade your landlord to paint the apartment.**
   a. "After three years we deserve some attention."
   b. "It wouldn't cost much, compared to what we pay in rent."
   c. "Maybe I could do some of the painting myself."
   d. "My boss is coming to dinner next week. He's bringing lots of new people into town—potential tenants."
   e. "I'd paint it if I were you—this isn't the only apartment in town."

2. **You're trying to quiet a noisy drunk at a party.**
   a. "Think what you'll feel like tomorrow!"
   b. "There's a very interesting girl over there. Sober up a little and I'll introduce you."
   c. "Can't you see, everybody is getting worried about you?"
   d. "You're too loud. Shut up."
   e. "I just heard you won the golf tournament. Tell me all about it."

3. **You're trying to talk the teacher into passing your teenage son—though she knows his homework papers were mostly done by you.**
   a. "But Tommy tries so hard. Can't you give him credit for effort?"

b. "The principal happens to be an old friend of mine!"

c. "I'm the one who goofed and I was wrong. Why not flunk *me* and give Tommy a chance to make it up?"

d. "My brother, the actor, is visiting and we'd like you to meet him."

e. "If Tommy only passes this course he'll get into a good college."

4. You're soliciting a charity donation from a thrifty prospect.

a. "Give me $10 and I'll fix the receipt so you can deduct $25 from your income tax."

b. "Don't you agree it's better to take care of our needs locally, so the government won't have to step in and raise taxes?"

c. "It's your civic duty, you know."

d. "If *you* give, my collection record will be perfect."

e. "This is a very worthy cause!"

5. A hoodlum sticks a gun in your back, and you're trying to save your money.

a. "You're out of luck. I left my wallet in my other suit."

b. "Watch out, buddy, I just graduated from karate school."

c. "Gee, I worked all week for that money!"

d. "Please! I can't face my wife if I come home broke."

e. "My wallet is in my hip pocket."

6. You've been promoted over an older employee and you want his cooperation.

a. "I'm going to need your help to get this job done."

b. "My new boss will be retiring soon, and when I get his job I'll put you in this one."

c. "Sorry I was promoted over you. You really deserved the job."

d. "Now I'm boss and you'll just have to do things my way."

e. "Look at it as a fresh opportunity to show how good you are."

7. **You're trying to get your boy to practice the piano when he wants to watch TV.**

   a. "You'll make me so proud if you learn to play well."

   b. "Be a good kid. We all have to do things we dislike."

   c. "Let's make a deal. If I let you watch this show, will you practice when it's over, without complaining?"

   d. "If you learn to play well, think how popular you'll be."

   e. "All that money for lessons will be wasted if you don't practice."

8. **You need your secretary to work overtime, but she has a date.**

   a. "Cancel this date, and I'll buy you the best steak in town when you finish this report."

   b. "The chief told me I just have to get this report out today."

   c. "I know it's an imposition—but *please*."

   d. "It's either stay and finish this, or back to the stenographers pool."

   e. "You're the only one I'd trust to do this right."

9. **You're trying to sell your husband on a second honeymoon.**

   a. "I saw Dr. Mason today, and he said you've *got* to get some rest."

   b. "You take a lot of business trips. Now I want a trip."

   c. "Doesn't ten days on a Caribbean island sound tempting?"

   d. "Gee, honey, I'd really love a vacation."

   e. "Wouldn't it be great—just the two of us alone together?"

10. **You're trying to talk a policeman out of giving you a ticket.**

   a. "Give me a break—this once."

   b. "Listen, would this five-dollar bill square things?"

   c. "Believe it or not, I've never had a ticket before."

   d. "I guess I was going pretty fast, and just didn't realize it."

   e. "I'm on my way to an important appointment and I just can't be late."

Brain Teasers 50

1. What is it that occurs once in a second, once in a month, once in a century, yet not at all in a year or week?

2. A bookkeeper noticed there were two consecutive double letters in the word *balloon*. She found other examples, such as *woolly* and *spittoon*. Then she tried to think of a word with three consecutive pairs of double letters. She couldn't think of any. Can you?

ROBIN MARCHAND

What Do You See? 51

What do you make out of the above design? Are you one of the few people who immediately see exactly what it is? Some recognize it in a few minutes; others never get it until told. There are no tricks—but this intriguing puzzle demonstrates how blind we can be to what we see.

LEON S. RHODES

Twist a Word 52

BEN L. O'DELL

Each definition below calls for a familiar common word. However, all members of a quartet of words must consist of the *same letters,* used the same number of times, but in different arrangements. For example:

(a) Airplane maneuvers .... LOOPS

(b) One-masted vessel .... SLOOP

(c) Small ponds of water .... POOLS

(d) A cylinder for thread .... SPOOL

To score yourself a right answer, you must provide words for all four definitions; six right is a passing grade; eight or more is excellent.

1. (a) Peril; hazard
   (b) Vegetable plot
   (c) Male goose
   (d) Moved within limits

2. (a) A tufted ornament
   (b) Grows rancid
   (c) Purloins
   (d) Small blackboards

3. (a) An expression of sorrow
   (b) Fireplace ledge
   (c) A long cloak
   (d) Pertaining to the mind

4. (a) Took an oath
   (b) A planter
   (c) Those in debt
   (d) Bad; ill (comparative)

5. (a) Animal's den
   (b) Metal track
   (c) Prevaricator
   (d) Seed covering

6. (a) Vipers
   (b) Totals again
   (c) Fears greatly
   (d) More sorrowful

7. (a) Football tosser
   (b) Not dense; scattered
   (c) Long-shafted weapons
   (d) Bowling term (plural)

8. (a) Kind of cheese
   (b) Woman (slang)
   (c) A meadow
   (d) Manufactured

9. (a) More pliant
   (b) Wooded area
   (c) Cherish; care for
   (d) Talent; strong point (plural)

10. (a) Fail to keep
    (b) Part of a shoe
    (c) Kind of gin drink
    (d) Name for a lion (plural)

Boil It Down 53

In the following string of letters, a logical sentence may be obtained by removing all unnecessary letters:

AALLLOUGNINCEACELSSSEANRYTELNETCTEERS

GERARD MOSLER

What's Your Energy I.Q.? 54

JAMES A. COX

You've read all those tips about saving energy—but how much of it has really sunk in? Take this quiz and find out. There are some curve-ball statements here, so think carefully before responding with a True or a False.

1. A thermostat setting of 68 degrees for your heating plant and air conditioner will give you a steady, healthy, year-round temperature and also save energy.

2. When you take a shower instead of a bath you always use less hot water.

3. If you live in a warm southern climate, you don't have to worry about insulating your home, installing storm sash, caulking and weather stripping around windows and doors.

4. Using your fireplace is not a sure-fire way of saving fuel.

5. Insulated draperies will actually prevent the sun from helping to heat your house on bright days.

6. Turn out all the lights when you leave a room, even if you'll be back shortly.

7. For efficiency, you should always run your dishwasher all the way through its dry cycle.

8. Operating your electric clothes washer, dryer and dishwasher at less than full capacity reduces motor strain, and results in fuel savings.

9. If your oven is big enough, you can cook a whole meal in it—roast, potatoes, vegetables—at one time.

10. Synthetic fabrics, including double-knits and permanent press, will dry just as well hanging from a line in your yard as in your dryer.

11. Some television sets use electricity even when turned off.

12. Keeping your freezer packed to capacity will save electricity.

13. You should consolidate your heavy household energy use—washers, dryers and so on—in the daylight hours, when utility companies are geared up to meet peak power demands.

14. Keeping heavy items in the trunk of your car will improve traction and give you better gasoline mileage.

15. Using your auto air conditioner doesn't waste energy so long as your engine is running fast enough to put power back into your battery.

16. Starting your car five minutes before you plan to use it and letting the engine warm up will circulate the oil, resulting in greater efficiency and less fuel burned.

17. Jackrabbit starts and screeching stops, "exercising" the gas pedal instead of keeping your foot steady on it, and not maintaining your speed while climbing a hill are all gasoline wasters.

18. Properly inflated tires, a tuned-up engine and correctly aligned wheels all help to conserve gasoline.

19. Although radial tires give you many more miles of service, they cause your car to burn more gasoline because they are underinflated compared with standard tires.

20. Using oil a grade or two heavier than that recommended by the automobile manufacturer will make your engine run "tighter" and help you save fuel.

Bird Calls 55

Just for a lark, try matching the definitions on the left with the appropriate bird names on the right. Don't duck this cardinal quiz.

1.	In golf, two below par on a hole	a. Adjutant
2.	Tool for opening hard-shelled fruits	b. Oriole
3.	To lose courage	c. Chat
4.	Wide-brimmed, shallow-crowned hat	d. Crane
5.	To peddle wares by crying them	e. Darter
6.	Toy to fly in the wind	f. Eagle
7.	To grumble	g. Goose
8.	Military officer's assistant	h. Grouse
9.	To shoot at individuals from hiding	i. Hawk
10.	Capable of moving at great speed	j. Kite
11.	Hoisting machine	k. Nutcracker
12.	In bridge, to trump a trick	l. Pigeon
13.	Tailor's long-handled pressing iron	m. Quail
14.	To use abusive language	n. Rail
15.	In show business, unsuccessful production	o. Ruff
16.	To converse informally	p. Skimmer
17.	One who is easily swindled (slang)	q. Snipe
18.	To devour	r. Swallow
19.	One who moves suddenly and swiftly	s. Swift
20.	Baltimore baseball player	t. Turkey

Word Gallery

ROBERT CAROLA

Here's a different way to have fun with words.
Study this collection of "word pictures," then
see what you can add to the list:

CL!MAX

ALON   E

KISS

LOWCUT   EXXTRA

cockeyed

YOGA

lift   balloon

ASTIGMATISM

NONCON𝓕ORMIST

QUICKSAND

Size Up Your
Reasoning Power 57

WILLIAM BERNARD AND JULES LEOPOLD

These self-administered examinations are fun to do—if you don't worry too much how you come out. Whip out a pencil and see if you are as bright as you always thought you were.

PART ONE:

DIRECTIONS—In each series, certain numbers or letters are left out. Insert the missing numbers or letters. For example: In 2, 4, 6, __, 10, __, 14, you should insert 8 in the first blank and 12 in the second. In A B C __ E __ G, you shoud insert D and F.

TIME LIMIT: 8 MINUTES

1. 3, 5, _, 9, 11, _, 15
2. Z X Y __ W __ U
3. A C E __ I K __
4. 100, __, 400, 800
5. Y E L __ O W
6. 9, 7, 11, __, 13, 11, _, 13
7. __, __, 9, 27, 81, __
8. 6, 8, 9, _, 12, _, 15
9. __, 24, 29, __, 33, 34, 35
10. A __ Z Y C D X __ E F __
11. 2, __, 2000, 2000, 200

PART TWO:

DIRECTIONS—Fill the blank squares with numbers which will make both the vertical columns and the horizontal rows in each diagram add up to the sum shown at the right of that diagram. Use no number larger than 9. Do not use zero.

TIME LIMIT: 3 MINUTES

A

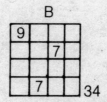

B

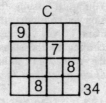

C

PART THREE:

DIRECTIONS—This is a list of birds, but the letters have been scrambled. Unscramble the letters and in the blank spaces write the words they spell. EGOSO, for example, when unscrambled spells GOOSE.

TIME LIMIT: 2 MINUTES

1. .... C K U D
2. .... L U L G
3. .... N O B R I
4. .... W R O C
5. .... N H E
6. .... N O P E I G
7. .... W K H A
8. .... L O W
9. .... R O R T A P
10. .... W A R P S O R
11. .... G E E L A
12. .... K H I E C C N
13. .... L E U B B R D I
14. .... B B R C L I K D A
15. .... K R O T S

PART FOUR:

DIRECTIONS—Each set of statements is followed by one or more conclusions. You are to assume that the statements are correct. Any conclusion you consider true and logical according to the statements, mark T. Any conclusion you consider not necessarily true according to the statements, mark F. For example: I am taller than John, John is taller than Joe. Therefore 1... T ... *I am taller than Joe.*

TIME LIMIT: 10 MINUTES

1. My secretary isn't old enough to vote. My secretary has beautiful hair. Therefore:

   1. ..... *My secretary is a girl under 18 years of age.*

II. Few stores on this street have neon lights, but they all have awnings. Therefore:

    1..... *Some have either awnings or neon lights.*
    2..... *Some have both awnings and neon lights.*

III. Potatoes are cheaper than tomatoes. I don't have enough money to buy two pounds of potatoes. Therefore:

    1..... *I haven't enough money to buy a pound of tomatoes.*
    2..... *I may or may not have enough to buy a pound of tomatoes.*

IV. Squares are shapes with angles. This shape has no angles. Therefore:

    1..... *This shape is a circle.*
    2..... *Any conclusion is uncertain.*
    3..... *This shape is not a square.*

V. Greenville is northeast of Smithtown. New York is northeast of Smithtown. Therefore:

    1..... *New York is closer to Greenville than to Smithtown.*
    2..... *Smithtown is southwest of New York.*
    3..... *New York is near Smithtown.*

VI. You are in your car, and if you stop short you will be hit by a truck behind you. If you don't stop short, you will hit a woman crossing the road. Therefore:

    1..... *Pedestrians should keep off the roads.*
    2..... *The truck is going too fast.*
    3..... *You will be hit by the truck or you will hit the woman.*

VII. B platoon attacked the enemy and was wiped out, maybe. Smith, a member of B platoon, recovered in base hospital. Therefore:

    1..... *The rest of B platoon was wiped out.*
    2..... *All of B platoon was wiped out.*
    3..... *All of B platoon was not wiped out.*

Are You a Good 58
Judge of Character?

JOHN KORD LAGEMANN

In sizing people up we all fall back now and
then on certain outward signs of inner character. You can check up on the accuracy of your
character readings by marking each of the
following common beliefs "true" or "false."

1. Long, slender hands mean an artistic temperament.

2. Redheaded people are more temperamental than other
   people.

3. A slow learner remembers what he has learned better than a
   fast learner.

4. A person who does not look you in the eye is likely to be
   dishonest.

5. Blondes are apt to be less trustworthy than brunettes.

6. Fat people are typically good-natured.

7. Wrinkles at the outer corners of the eyes show that a person
   has a sense of humor.

8. Curly hair is a symptom of exuberance and vitality.

9. A high, bulging forehead is a sign of superior brainpower.

10. Cold hands are a sign of affectionate disposition.

More Kangaroo Words 59

BEN L. O'DELL

A kangaroo word (see Test 6) carries within its spelling, in normal order, a smaller word that is a perfect synonym for itself. For example, note how the word BLOSSOMS contains the word BLOOMS. See if you can find the synonym hiding in each word below.

1. EVACUATE
2. ENCOURAGE
3. PROSECUTE
4. CALUMNIES
5. RAPSCALLION
6. INDOLENT
7. PRATTLE
8. DIVERSIFIED
9. RAMPAGE
10. MATCHES

11. PERAMBULATE
12. PINIONED
13. JOVIALITY
14. CONTAINER
15. REGULATES
16. SPLOTCHES
17. SLITHERED
18. PERIMETER
19. CURTAIL
20. RESPITE

Fascinating Fact Quiz 60

DAVID LOUIS

1. Which bounces higher, a ball of steel or a ball of rubber?

2. A raisin dropped in a glass of fresh champagne will move up and down continuously. Will it do the same in beer?

3. Why does a whip crack?

4. Lightning strikes the earth: a) 1000 times an hour. b) 100 times a minute. c) 100 times a second.

5. An egg, set spinning, may rise up on end. What if anything does that indicate?

6. Do you get enough calories from a piece of celery to replace the calories spent in eating it?

7. How much nourishment in the glue on a postage stamp: a) a full calorie. b) a half calorie. c) a tenth of a calorie.

8. How many pounds of food and drink does the average person ingest in a year?

9. How fast does a sneeze travel?

10. On a clear moonless night, from atop a mountain peak, you can see a match struck how many miles away:...5 ...20...50.

11. On which of your hands do the fingernails grow faster?

12. It takes 17 muscles to smile. To frown takes:...13... 17...29...43.

13. The average human heart beats how many times in a 72-year lifespan?

14. Statues of heroes on horseback sometimes show the horse rearing. Is it simply a matter of sculptor's choice?

15. There are many ways to play the ten opening moves in chess. *How* many? a) millions. b) billions. c) trillions. d) even more.

16. "Googol" means an enormous number. Can you define it more precisely?

17. Of all names in the world, which is most common?

18. There was once (in 1788) a state in the U.S.A. called Franklin. Today it's part of _____.

19. "Jackdaws love my big sphinx of quartz." Anything remarkable about that sentence?

20. How many muscles does a caterpillar have: a) 1500. b) 2000. c) 2500.

21. In one night a mole can tunnel: a) 50 feet. b) 100 feet. c) 300 feet.

22. What's the fastest fish in the sea?

23. How many quills on a porcupine? a) 12,000. b) 24,000. c) 36,000.

24. What color combination has the strongest visual impact?

25. The greatest number of phone calls ever handled in one U.S. city during a 24-hour period was 80 million. It happened in New York. Can you guess when, on what occasion?

26. How many advertisements is the average American exposed to in a day: a) 50. b) 100. c) 300. d) 500.

27. For the Louisiana Purchase lands, the U.S.A. paid France less than three cents an acre. What did it pay Russia, per acre, for Alaska?

28. Americans spend more than a billion dollars a year on sneakers. True or False?

How Do You Tell You're in Love? 61

LESTER DAVID

Millions of teen-agers ask the question: "How will I know I'm in love?" As Dr. David R. Mace, executive director of the American Association of Marriage Counselors, put it: "It's always difficult to know for sure—especially when you're young."

This quiz was prepared after extensive consultations with experts who have made wide-scale studies of this wonderful yet mysterious emotion. It should help a young person make that all-important decision: "Is it love—or something else?" Check *Yes* only if you have quite definite feelings about your answer. If there's some doubt in your mind, check *No*.

1. Did this thing happen all of a sudden?

YES   NO

2. Would you be very jealous and upset if someone else made a serious play for him or her?

YES   NO

3. When you aren't together, do you find yourself mooning around, unable to do much except sigh over your beau or belle?

YES   NO

4. Are you more in love when you are together than when you are by yourself?

YES   NO

5. Do you honestly feel that the boy or girl is just about the Most Perfect Person in the world?

YES   NO

6. Are you, on the whole, pretty unhappy at home with your parents?

YES   NO

7. Do you know how your heart-throb feels about money and children?

YES   NO

8. Do you find that, when it comes to this particular boy or girl, you are always anxious to appear at your best—that you are conscious about what you say and how you look and act?

YES   NO

9. Most people agree that there cannot be real love unless two persons share common interests. But how about common miseries? Do both of you have a substantial number of complaints in common about homes, parents, school and other things in your lives?

YES   NO

10. Suppose your beloved has gone on an extended trip and written you beautiful and affectionate letters. Would you show these around in your group?

YES   NO

Not So Easy 62

CEDRIC ADAMS

How quickly can you find out what's unusual about this paragraph? It looks so ordinary you'd think nothing was wrong with it at all—and, in fact, nothing is. But it *is* unusual. Why? Study it, think about it, and you may find out. But you must do it without coaching: I'm not going to assist you in any way. No doubt, if you work at it for a bit, it will dawn on you. Who knows until you try? So hop to it, try your skill and pray for luck. Par is about half an hour.

77

Word Play 63

1. Can you, using the same five letters, spell two words that have exactly opposite meanings? Both begin with "u."

BRIAN HALL

2. What seven-letter word contains eight words without rearranging any of its letters?

HELEN M. MORAND

3. What word in the English language has three dotted letters in a row?

GAINES BREWSTER

4. What word has eight letters and only one vowel?

PAUL D. PEERY

5. The word "startling" can be changed into eight other familiar words by successive deletions, from different places, of one letter at a time. Remember that you can't put a letter back once you've taken it out.

MARTIN GARDNER

6. What word, starting with a consonant, is trailed by four vowels?

BRIAN HALL

7. What words contain such unlikely combinations of letters as tomo, xyg, dhp, zop, heon, riju, xop, and omaha?

BENNETT CERF

What One Word II

BEN L. O'DELL

Here's another game designed to limber up your vocabulary. You are challenged to find a *single word* which will be a synonym for *both* the two radically different words in each number that follows. You should be able to supply at least 11 of these double-duty words, but 14 or more is excellent.

1. Skin-Conceal
2. Pull-Sketch
3. Peevish-Buggy
4. Saloon-Obstruct
5. Pillage-Bag
6. Stumble-Journey
7. Rasp-Column
8. Hill-Horse
9. Lease-Tear
10. Crate-Spar
11. Courage-Pick
12. Custom-Costume
13. Musket-Rob
14. Handbag-Pucker
15. Drama-Romp
16. Encounter-Proper
17. Dismiss-Shoot
18. Acrobats-Glasses

Try This Mystery Quiz 65

CHARLES D. RICE

We're not going to tell you what this quiz is all about until you've taken it. Grab a pencil and write in the answers as fast as you can. Don't worry if you have to leave some answers blank. The only rule is, don't peek at the answers until you've finished.

A. He's opening the **B.** Frilly gadget is **C.** Junior's riding a

G. These golf-pants are **H.** This machine is a **I.** They're sitting in a

D. This timepiece is a   **E.** His hair style is a   **F.** Drums are called

J. Cop is twirling a   **K.** What's this called?   **L.** What style of tie?

Numbers Game 66

LAWRENCE B. BIXBY

Ethiopian tribesmen, travelers say, can only double or halve numbers, and that only by using pebbles as counters. Yet merely by halving and doubling, they take any two numbers, multiply them and come out with the right answer. Say a tribesman wants to buy 15 sheep at 13 Ethiopian dollars each. How much is that? Here's how he goes about finding out. Put 13 in a left column, 15 on the right. Halve the left figure; you get 6½. Ignore the ½; Ethiopians don't know anything about fractions. Double the right-hand figure. Keep this up until the left-hand figure is 1. Now you have:

13	15
6	30
3	60
1	120

Even numbers in the left column are evil, the superstitious tribesmen say, and must be destroyed, along with their guilty partners. So scratch out 6 and its partner 30. Now add the right-hand column and you have the right answer: 195. Try it with any two numbers; it does not matter which is halved or doubled; the answer is always right. The Ethiopian's primitive mind simply cannot grasp how our system works. Of course you see at once how *his* works. Or do you?

The World's Easiest Quiz 67

DAVID WALLECHINSKY AND IRVING WALLACE

At first glance, the questions below seem to belong in the "Who is buried in Grant's Tomb?" category. With one exception, they are not. A passing grade requires seven correct answers.

1. How long did the Hundred Years War last?

2. In which country are Panama hats made?

3. Where do we get catgut?

4. What are moleskin trousers made of?

5. Louis XVIII was the last one, but how many previous kings of France were called Louis?

6. What kind of creatures were the Canary Isles named after?

7. What was King George VI's first name?

8. What color is a purple finch?

9. What is a camel's-hair brush made of?

10. How long did the Thirty Years War last?

Man or Woman? 68

LESTER DAVID

Is it possible to tell a man from a woman by their reactions to everyday situations? It is—for a psychologist. But how about you? Test your knowledge of men-women differences on these questions based on studies.

1. Two persons dip into a box of chocolates. One eats the entire piece at once; the other bites it to see what is inside. Who's the biter?   Man____   Woman____

2. At a party, a guest says that most people don't want to visit the moon. One listener agrees, citing opinion surveys. Another disagrees, asserting: "I don't think that's true, *I* want to go." Who judges other people's reactions this way?   Man____   Woman____

3. A husband and wife are in the living room reading, while their sick baby is asleep upstairs. One of them looks up and says: "You're worrying abut the baby, aren't you? The doctor says he'll be fine." Who was first to perceive the other's concern?   Man____   Woman____

4. A man and wife are dining in a restaurant. One orders unusual dishes the family has never tried before. The other sticks to more familiar fare. Who's the food adventurer?   Man____   Woman____

5. The same couple enter a
   shop. On one side is an array
   of new products; on the other is
   a display of familiar merchandise. Which one is fascinated
   by the newer items?   Man____   Woman____

6. Two shoppers go into a store
   for new clothes. One asks for
   a particular garment and color.
   But who just asks vaguely to
   see some clothes?   Man____   Woman____

7. The car's gas gauge is danger-
   ously low. One person in the
   car wants to stop right away
   and fill up. The other wants
   to make it across the bridge to
   where gas is cheaper. Which is
   the chance-taker?   Man____   Woman____

8. En route to a strange destina-
   tion, a couple realize that
   they're lost. One wants to ask
   directions, the other to cruise
   around looking. Who's the
   cruiser?   Man____   Woman____

9. The gas-station attendant
   asks, "Check your oil and
   water?" This motorist says: "Not
   now, I'm in a hurry." The
   driver's spouse, however,
   waits for the checkup. Who
   won't wait?   Man____   Woman____

10. Three cars are stopped
    abreast for a red light. As
    the signal turns green, one
    tries to beat the others to
    a getaway. Who's the drag
    racer?   Man____   Woman____

Bonus Question

11. An especially sad movie
    comes to the neighborhood.
    Who will feel sadder as the
    tearful scenes unreel?   Man____   Woman____

Are You a Shrewd Driver? 69

C. LESTER WALKER

Say you're at the wheel of a car. Do you know what to do if your brakes fail going downhill, or an oncoming car swerves out of control into your lane? Research by highway patrols, universities and insurance companies has established beyond dispute the best maneuvers in such emergencies. They aren't necessarily one's instinctive response. But they can be *learned* by being practiced in the imagination over and over again.

Test yourself on the eight emergency situations described here.

1. You're going 60. Suddenly, *bang!*—followed by a violent tug to the right on your steering wheel. Your right front tire has blown out. What do you do?

2. Driving about 50 at night, you come unexpectedly upon a sharp, unbanked curve to the right. As you try to angle into it, you sense that the curve is too sharp for you to hold the car on the road.

3. Rolling downhill, gaining speed, you step on your brake pedal. It "mushes" lifelessly to the floor—no brakes!

4. A traffic light on the highway ahead turns red faster than you expected, and you stop quickly. Behind you, brakes screech. In your mirror you glimpse a truck. In a couple of seconds it's going to plow into the rear of your car.

5. A farm truck shoots out of a lane on the right and starts across the road directly in front of you. You've been doing 50, and are almost on him.

6. Going 50 on wet blacktop, you try to dodge a hole in the pavement. The rear of your car starts skidding hard to the right.

7. A car, trying to pass you, forces you to swerve right. Your right wheels drop over the edge of the pavement onto the soft shoulder several inches below. You're doing 60.

8. An oncoming car zigzags into your lane on a two-lane highway and, weaving slightly, suddenly heads like a missile directly for you.

Cash in Hand 70

1. A quarter has 119 grooves on its circumference. How many grooves on a dime?

DAVID LOUIS

2. On a new five-dollar bill, how many state names can you make out?

JOHN L. EDWARDS

3. How many times can a dollar bill be folded, each fold halving it so one side neatly overlaps the other?

DAVID LOUIS

4. If you find a star in front of the serial number on a bill in your pocket, what does it mean?

Nature-Fact or Nature-Fiction?

71

ALAN DEVOE

If you can answer correctly seven questions in the following quiz, your ability to distinguish nature facts from superstitious beliefs is better than that of most people; if 10 or more, your nature lore is exceptional.

1. A wild animal is more likely to attack you if you are afraid of it.   T—   F—
2. Only the female mosquito ever bites you.   T—   F—
3. Moss grows thickest on the north side of trees.   T—   F—
4. A chameleon takes on the color of the object on which it rests.   T—   F—
5. A person who cannot hear at all is deaf as an adder.   T—   F—
6. Summer is warmer than winter because the earth is then nearer the sun.   T—   F—
7. Beavers use their tails as trowels when building their dams.   T—   F—
8. Venomous snakes are immune to their own poison.   T—   F—
9. Horned toads squirt blood out of their eyes.   T—   F—
10. If you cut an earthworm in two, each half will become a new worm.   T—   F—
11. A shark must turn belly-up in order to bite.   T—   F—
12. Elephants live to be several hundred years old.   T—   F—
13. Squirrels have an accurate memory for the places where they have buried nuts.   T—   F—

Can You Fill In the O's? 72

BORIS RANDOLPH

Each group of letters below is a perfect word—except that three or four "o's" have been left out. Just fill them in and see how many you can complete correctly. Example: Given the letters CTTNWD, you can fill in four "o's" and get the word cottonwood.

1. VD
2. SNRUS
3. FFSHT
4. CTRN
5. PRTCL
6. LKUT
7. MNTNUS
8. STRERM
9. RATRI
10. CRRBRATR
11. SCILGY
12. DUBLN
13. BH
14. DRUS
15. RCC
16. FRENN
17. LNG
18. FTLSE
19. RTHDX
20. HMLGUS

Alphabetease 73

FRANK FREEMAN

An old church in Wales has a mysterious inscription carved over the door above the Ten Commandments. A scholar discovered that, by adding a single letter, and only that letter, throughout the phrase, it made sense. So try your own decoding skill on:

PRSVRYPRFCTMN
VRKPTHSPRCPTSTN

Judge for Yourself! 74

ALBERT W. FRIBOURG AND DAVID STEIN

The following legal problems are from 61 actual U.S. cases assembled in the book "Judge for Yourself!" by lawyers Fribourg and Stein. They provide an excellent test of your wits. Consider the facts, and the principle of law involved, then check your own decision against that made by the judge.

SORE THUMB

FACTS: When Thomas Garland was mugged and robbed, his most serious injury was a cut on his thumb. But the surgeon he consulted told him that unless the thumb was amputated immediately his life was in danger. Garland refused to take the advice.

At the end of two weeks, lockjaw developed, and the thumb had to be amputated. Then it was too late, and Garland died.

The robber was indicted for murder. At the trial, the doctor testified that had the thumb been amputated promptly, Garland would not have died.

PROBLEM: Should Garland's neglect send the prisoner to Death Row?

THE CHERRY TREE

FACTS: The trunk of Sarah Hoffman's cherry tree stood two feet from the border line separating her farm from Abner Armstrong's. The limbs of the tree, however, extended over the line. When the fruit was ripe, Sarah picked cherries from the limbs above her own property and then leaned over to take fruit from the limbs hanging over Abner's farm. At that moment Abner came along and a fight ensued.

LAW: The owner of land owns it upward to the sky and downward to the center of the earth.

PROBLEM: Who gets the cherries on the overhanging limbs?

THE SPECIALIST

FACTS: Anna Mohr's right ear ached so badly that when the specialist advised an operation she readily assented. Before she was anesthetized, Anna Mohr believed that the specialist would operate on her right ear. Great was her astonishment when she discovered that he had actually operated on the left one.

The specialist explained that before starting the operation he had examined both ears, and found the left one in more urgent need of an operation. The patient's family physician was present at the operation, and knew of the change of plan. Everyone agreed the operation had been successful, and skillfully performed; nevertheless the patient sued the doctor.

LAW: An unauthorized touching of another's person is an assault and battery—for which damages may be recovered.

PROBLEM: Was Anna Mohr entitled to damages because the specialist cut the left ear without bringing her out of the anesthesia and obtaining her consent?

THUMBED NOSES

FACTS: On several occasions Morris Garstenfeld publicly thumbed his nose at John Shannon, and the latter had him arrested for disorderly conduct.

LAW: Any person who, with intent to provoke a breach of the peace or whereby a breach of the peace may be occasioned, "uses offensive, disorderly, threatening, abusive or insulting language, conduct or behavior..." shall be deemed guilty of disorderly conduct.

PROBLEM: Would the application of "the thumb of his right hand to the end of his nose," and then executing "an aerial flourish with his fingers" occasion a breach of the peace?

"MARRY IN HASTE..."

FACTS: Mr. and Mrs. Mirizio were married in a civil ceremony in September. Both being Catholics, they agreed they would not live together until after a church wedding, to take place at Christmas. Christmas came, but the husband did not appear for the ceremony.

The wife sued for separation and demanded alimony. She said she was willing to make a home for her husband, but would not cohabit with him until after a church ceremony. Mirizio refused to support a wife in name only.

LAW: If, without just cause, a wife refused to cohabit with her husband, he need not support her.

PROBLEM: Was Mirizio justified in refusing to support Mrs. Mirizio?

KOSHER BACON

FACTS: "These progressive dealers sell Armour's Star Bacon in the new window-top carton." Thus read an Armour advertisement, and in the list was the name of Max Braun, a kosher butcher.

Braun called this libel, and sued. Armour & Co. moved to dismiss his complaint, claiming that they had nothing to gain by the statement and further that the language used was complimentary for they had called Braun a "progressive" dealer.

LAW: The publication of a false writing which would injure the reputation of a person or expose him to ridicule or contempt is libel.

PROBLEM: Should Braun collect?

The Spy in the Rust-Colored Coat 75

SUSAN ZIVICH

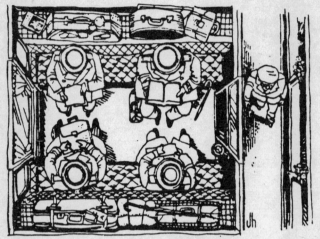

1. Four spies in trench coats sat in four facing seats

2. As they traveled the Peking Express.

3. With two by the window and two by the aisle,

4. The arrangement was strange (as you guessed):

5. The English spy sat on Mr. B's left.

6. Mr. A had a coat colored tan.

7. The spy dressed in olive was on the German spy's right.

8. Mr. C was the only cigar-smoking man.

9. Mr. D was across from the American spy.

10. The Russian, in khaki, had a scarf round his throat.

11. The English spy stared out the window on his left.

12. So who was the spy in the rust-colored coat?

How Much Do You Know About Men? 76

AMRAM SCHEINFELD

Women have always believed they understand men better than men understand them. Perhaps they do. Decide which of the following statements is true, which false—always remembering that we are talking in terms of *averages*. If you're right on seven of the answers, you'll be doing very well.

1. Men's bodies are constructed more perfectly and efficiently than women's.   T—   F—
2. Men age more rapidly than women.   T—   F—
3. Tests have proved that men and women have the same intelligence.   T—   F—
4. Men are less emotional than women.   T—   F—
5. Men are less likely to be hysterical than women.   T—   F—
6. Faced with menacing problems or great suffering, men are more likely to commit suicide than women.   T—   F—
7. Men see color less well.   T—   F—
8. Men can't stand heat and cold, or severe exposure, as well as women.   T—   F—
9. Men's senses are less delicate than women's.   T—   F—
10. Men are generally inferior to women in manual dexterity.   T—   F—
11. Men inherit more talent for art and music.   T—   F—
12. Men sleep more soundly than women.   T—   F—
13. Men are less intuitive.   T—   F—

Translation, Please 77

PERSIS CAMPBELL

Can you turn the following string of numbers into a meaningful English sentence: 100204180.

Hit or Myth? 78

CHARLIE RICE

You're not supposed to know the answers to the following eight questions—just size up the situation and make a guess. After you're through, we'll tell you what your score suggests about your personality.

1. What did Nero do when Rome burned?
   - ☐ a He fiddled.
   - ☐ b He fled to his summer palace outside the city.
   - ☐ c He opened a Fire Relief Fund afterward and demanded contributions.

2. Lemmings are small rodents that inhabit Sweden and Norway. What is the truth about them?
   - ☐ a Each year, lemmings march to the sea and commit deliberate mass suicide by drowning.
   - ☐ b Some years, migrating on a straight-line course, lemmings march to the sea, swim on out and drown.
   - ☐ c Lemmings are strictly city rodents and never march anywhere.

3. George Washington is supposed to have cut down a cherry tree and said to his father, "I cannot tell a lie—I did it." What do you think?
- ☐ a Basically true.
- ☐ b Possibly true.
- ☐ c Not credible.

4. What is your judgment about the tale that Lady Godiva rode naked through the streets of Coventry to protest her cruel husband's tax on the populace?
- ☐ a Probably true.
- ☐ b Highly unlikely.
- ☐ c Absolute nonsense.

5. In the *Titanic* disaster, what was the orchestra playing when the ship went down?
- ☐ a "Nearer, My God, to Thee."
- ☐ b "Autumn."
- ☐ c Dance music.

6. How many of each animal did Noah take aboard the Ark?
- ☐ a One pair of each animal.
- ☐ b Seven pairs of some animals, one pair of others.
- ☐ c Very few animals at all, since the Ark was a small craft by present-day standards.

7. Which statement do you believe?
- ☐ a Abe Lincoln was the only President born in a log cabin.
- ☐ b Three Presidents were born in log cabins.
- ☐ c More than half a dozen Presidents were born in log cabins.

8. William Tell, Arthur of Camelot and "Casey at the Bat" are all well-known. How many really existed?
- ☐ a All three.
- ☐ b Only Arthur.
- ☐ c None of them.

Questions for Young People, and for Parents

LESTER DAVID

How are communications between the genera-
tions in your family? Here is a double-barreled
quiz to help you find out. Note: The questions
may seem simple, but don't be fooled. They
touch matters of importance.

PART ONE:

PARENTS—QUIZ THE TEENS

1. Does Father prefer coffee before a meal, with it or after it?
2. Is Dad a pro-football fan? If so, what team does he root for?
3. How did Mother and Dad meet? Did they have a long or a short engagement?
4. What month is Mother's Day? Father's Day?
5. Name one of Mother's girlhood movie idols.
6. Name one of Father's boyhood sports heroes.
7. (For boys) What does it cost, within $3, to run the car each month? (For girls) What, within $3, is the family's monthly telephone bill?
8. If Dad served in the armed forces: What branch was he in? What rank did he reach?
9. Is Mother a member of the PTA?
10. Is Father good at math?
11. Did Father's family have a car when he was your age? Did Mother's?
12. Name two of Mother's good friends. And two of Father's.
13. If you plan to go to college, what will it cost to send you for one year? (Come reasonably close.)

14. You probably know your mother and dad's wedding anniversary date but was their wedding a large formal ceremony or a small intimate one?

15. Can you relate one funny or dramatic incident that happened to Mother or Dad before you were six?

16. Name a food Father can't stand.

17. Where does Father work? (Answer must be more specific than "downtown someplace"!)

18. Did you talk over at least one personal problem with either parent in the past two weeks?

19. When Mother was about your age, was she good at sports? Which ones?

20. Being a parent isn't easy. What do you suppose are the two biggest problems we have?

PART TWO:

TEENS—QUIZ YOUR PARENTS

1. Do I believe in God? How do I feel right now about my religion?

2. What part of the chicken do I like best?

3. If I had been old enough to vote in the last election, how would I have voted?

4. Do I want to go to college? If so, what are my top choices as of now?

5. Who is my best friend?

6. Do any of my teachers especially bug me?

7. Within 50 cents, what does it cost these days for a fellow to take a girl out on a movie-and-soda date?

8. Name four subjects I'm taking this term. Am I having trouble with any? If so, which one?

9. Am I a class officer? On any school athletic team? In any clubs or organizations in or out of school?

10. Was I sad or glad over the outcome of the World Series?

11. Say at least three words in current teen-age slang. (Or, teenagers, you say three now being used in your set and ask the folks what they mean.)

12. Am I doing a special report for any of my classes right now? If so, what about?

13. How much did I grow in the past year?
14. Have I had all my polio shots?
15. Within a half hour—how much time do I spend on my homework on an average evening?
16. Name three currently popular teen-age dances.
17. Did I pass all my subjects last term? If not, which did I fail?
18. Did I earn any money outside of my allowance in the past two weeks? If so, how much?
19. Did I go out last Saturday night? If so, with whom? About what time did I get home?
20. Being a teen-ager isn't easy. What do you suppose are the two biggest problems I have?

An "I.Q." Test 80

If you can complete all but one or two of these words containing the letters I and Q, your "I.Q." I.Q. is definitely superior!

-IQ------	=Cordials
---IQ---	=Made new item look old
--IQ--	=Sole
-IQ---	=Spurred
--IQ--	=Exclusive
-IQ---	=Card game for two
-IQ---	=Fluid
----IQ--	=Decorate with cutouts
-IQ------	=Spiciness
-IQ----	=Melt
--IQ------	=Propriety
-------IQ---	=Official announcements
---IQ---------	=Occurring twice in three months
-IQ---------	=Converting assets to cash
---IQ--	=Slanting
------IQ---	=Stanching device

Pick the Champs

How many of the animal champions can you name? If you get twelve right, you have something to brag about. Ten is good and eight is fair. But stay alert. Some of the questions are mildly tricky.

1. What is the largest animal living today?

2. What is the largest animal that ever lived?

3. What is the largest land animal of North America?

4. What is the largest bird in the world?

5. What is the longest snake in the world?

6. What bird has the greatest wingspread?

7. What animal lives the longest?

8. What mammal lives the longest?

9. What four-footed animal can run the fastest?

10. What is the largest of all deer?

11. What animal, next to man, is most intelligent?

12. What animal produces the world's finest fleece?

13. What wild animal is most helpful to man?

Lady in the Middle 82

Fill in the blank with a woman's name and make a word:

1. AB__LITY
2. SUM__S
3. O__CTIVE
4. A__TION

5. REA__E
6. S__NTY
7. BIG__
8. TIS__

Irish or English 83

To solve this time-honored test of reasoning power, you must first make the preposterous assumption that Englishmen *always* lie, and Irishmen *always* tell the truth.

You are rowing toward a shore on which stand three men. You shout to them: "Are you Irish or English?"

A man answers, but his words are blown away in the wind.

A second man cries: "He says he's Irish, and he *is*. So am I."

The third man cries: "He's English—but *I* am Irish."

What is the nationality of each of the three men?

Brain Busters 84

1. What five-letter word contains four personal pronouns, with the letters in the correct order?

J. HARRY BENSON

2. Make a single common English word from the following letters: *pnlleeeesssss*.

MARJ HEYDUCK

3. Add one vowel to the letters *wtthfl*, then unscramble them and make a word.

ARTIE SHAW

4. Fill in the blanks, using the same set of letters in the same order in each blank, and make a sensible sentence:
A _____ doctor was _____ to operate because he had _____

5. What word is made shorter by adding a syllable to it?

BENNETT CERF

For the Parlor Psychologist 85

Here are some conversation starters for the amateur analyst. The answers can be fun; they may also be significant. But first, answer the questions yourself, and check the interpretation in the back of the book.

1. What age would you like to be for the rest of your life?

2. If you lost everything you own what would you do?

3. If you were caught in a fire and could grab only one object, what would it be? (All family and pets are safe.)

4. If you could choose one place to live the rest of your life, where would it be?

5. If you had just 24 hours to live, how would you spend them?

6. If you were in a serious jam, to whom would you go for help?

The World's Cussedest Quiz 86

CHARLES D. RICE

Take a look at the questions below and you'll see they're as easy as rolling off a log. However, we'll bet you can't answer more than four correctly. If you can, you're in the genius class. The quiz has been tested on scores of persons, from taxi drivers to college professors. The average result was a little better than *two right!*

1. For what crime was Captain Kidd hanged?

2. To whose conception does the "Immaculate Conception" refer?

3. To what musical form does the anthem "My Country, 'Tis of Thee" belong? a. Tango b. Slow march c. Waltz d. Fox Trot

4. At which of the four seasons in the United States is the sun nearest the earth?

5. In World War I, who said to the French people, "Lafayette, we are here"?

6. There should be one comma in the title of the folk song "God Rest Ye Merry Gentlemen." After which word should it be placed?

7. Which of the following substances does a plant depend on for almost 100 percent of its food? a. Rock b. Air c. Soil d. Bacteria

8. How were "witches" put to death in early Salem, Mass.?

9. Which of the following phrases most accurately describes the word "Xmas"? a. An irreverent, commercialized form. b. An ancient, reverent form. c. A space-saving form invented by headline writers.

105

Could You Have Solved the Problem? 87

1. A woman rushed into a garage with her eight-year-old son, who had pushed a ball-bearing case shaped like a ring onto his finger and couldn't get it off. His mother had tried soap and water, then taken him to a hospital, finally had come to the garage to have it cut off. But the ring was made of specially hardened steel which the garage's files and hacksaws couldn't cut. By this time the finger was red and swollen. A man got the ring off in a few minutes. Can you guess how?

A. T. ANDERSON

2. One day I drove up a country lane, parked my car in the shade of a large tree and started toward a nearby house to make a business call. I was barely out of my car when a fierce dog lunged at me. Fortunately, he was chained to the tree and I managed to get out of his reach. Finding no one home, I walked back toward my car. The dog growled and lunged again. His chain was long, and my car was in such a position that he could easily cover both doors. So how did I get into my car without being touched by the animal?

LAWRENCE BOLZ

3. I was riding a frisky pony when his bridle worked loose. He promptly shook it off and started to gallop down the road, paying no attention to my commands to stop. I stuck on and hoped for the best, until a car loomed up ahead. I had to stop that pony—and I did. Can you suggest a way?

DOROTHY DICKS

4. One evening an insect flew into my ear too deep to reach. It started to crawl and buzz, sounding as if a twin-engine plane were operating in my head. Can you guess how I got it out?

JAMES H. CORWIN

Stung by a Spelling Bee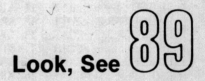

- An eccentric chap named Turner recently began signing his name Phtholognyrrh. Can you justify his bizarre orthography?

- Another fellow spells the name of a homely vegetable in this formidable way: ghoughphtheightteeau. Can you respell it to be more recognizable?

Look, See 89

1. Are you observant enough to detect the common characteristics of these six words: deft, sighing, calmness, canopy, first, stun?

BENNETT CERF

2. Rearrange these letters—OOUSWTDNERJ—to spell just one word. No proper name, nothing foreign or unusual.

GENE SHERMAN

Juggle Letters - II 90

BEN L. O'DELL

Once again, as in Test 7, you are asked to turn each pair of words into *synonyms* by taking a *single letter* from either word and placing it somewhere within the other one, without rearranging any other letters. As an illustration, by taking the R from SHRED and inserting it into BAN, you get SHED and BARN.

1. SHRED . . . . BAN
2. LAUGHTER . . . SKILL
3. FREIGHT . . . . . SCAR
4. SIT . . . . CULT
5. BOAST . . . . HIP
6. RIG . . . . PENAL
7. EGO . . . . LAVE
8. HOP . . . . CHEW
9. REGIMENT . . . . . . DIE
10. PANT . . . . SLOW

11. ARCHES . . . . . . HUTS
12. SPARS . . . . THINE
13. RALLY . . . . . . FIEND
14. STAY . . . . SATE
15. EAR . . . . TREND
16. ASSETS . . . . . RAVERS
17. BOOST . . . . HOE
18. ASK . . . . LIE
19. RATS . . . . . . RANGES
20. BLARE . . . . BAD

Mountains Out of Molehills 91

AARON SUSSMAN

Here are simple, familiar proverbs restated. Try to put them back into their original form.

1. Individuals who perforce are constrained to be domiciled in vitreous structures of patent frangibility should on no account employ petrous formations as projectiles.

2. That prudent avis which matutinally deserts the coziness of its abode will ensnare a vermiculate creature.

3. Everything that coruscates with effulgence is not *ipso facto* aurous.

4. Do not dissipate your competence by hebetudinous prodigality lest you subsequently lament an exiguous inadequacy.

5. An addlepated beetlehead and his specie divaricate with startling prematurity.

6. It can be no other than a maleficent horizontally propelled current of gaseous matter whose portentous advent is not the harbinger of a modicum of beneficence.

7. One should hyperesthetically exercise macrography upon that situs which one will eventually tenant if one propels oneself into the troposphere.

8. Aberration is the hallmark of homo sapiens, while longanimous placability and condonation are the indicia of supramundane omniscience.

How Masculine or Feminine Are You? 92

This quiz reflects observations by psychologists over many years, and—in a changing world—has a degree of validity still. Give yourself one point for every "A" answer, two for every "B."

1. Would you rather—(A) work for a pleasant boss; (B) work for yourself?

2. Which do you consider holds the greater hope for the world—(A) religion; (B) science?

3. Which do you like better—(A) music; (B) sports?

4. When buying a new car, which is more important to you—(A) design; (B) engine?

5. Do you prefer—(A) having decisions made for you: (B) to make your own?

6. Men are more successful because of their—(A) appearance; (B) capability?

7. Are your feelings often easily hurt—(A) yes; (B) no?

8. Which do you enjoy more—(A) poetry; (B) detective stories?

9. Have you a great fear of fire—(A) yes; (B) no?

10. Which interests you more—(A) art; (B) politics?

11. Does impolite language annoy you—(A) yes; (B) no?

12. Would you rather be—(A) conventional; (B) startling?

13. Which of these dogs would you rather own—(A) poodle; (B) boxer?

14. Do you like to go to parties and dances—(A) yes; (B) no?

15. Have you ever cried at sad movies—(A) yes; (B) no?

16. Do practical jokes annoy you—(A) yes; (B) no?

17. Which does a woman need more—(A) clothes; (B) intelligence?

18. Do you resent persons using nicknames—(A) yes; (B) no?

19. Would you rather—(A) sell in a store; (B) sell outside?

20. If your lights went out, would you—(A) call the electric company; (B) try to fix them yourself?

21. Do you like to buy antique furniture—(A) yes; (B) no?

22. Do you prefer mingling with people more intelligent than yourself—(A) yes; (B) no?

23. Is it hard for you to get up as soon as you awake—(A) yes; (B) no?

24. Does soiled table linen disgust you—(A) yes; (B) no?

25. Do you feel pity for a drowning bee—(A) yes; (B) no?

Pocket Calculations 93

1. My watch is ten minutes slow, though I'm under the impression it's five minutes fast. Your watch is five minutes fast, though you think it's ten minutes slow. We both plan to catch a four o'clock train. Who gets there first? Work this out mentally, without resorting to pencil and paper.

ANGUS REID

2. Man: How many birds and how many beasts do you have in this zoo?
Zookeeper: There are 30 heads and 100 feet.
Man: I can't tell from *that!*
Zookeeper: Oh, yes, you can. Just work it out.

JAMES F. FIXX

Contract Word Game

JACK BARRETT

The object is to reduce each word in length, one letter at a time, until you have reduced it as far as you can. Every letter deleted must leave a new word, one letter shorter; and the order of the letters must not be changed. Each letter removed counts one point. No. 1 has been filled in to show the procedure. The author totaled 56 points. Can you top that score?

1. THOROUGH: through, though, tough. . . . .
2. MORON . . . .
3. NATIVE . . . .
4. BEREFT . . . .
5. MANAGER . . . .
6. CRACKLED . . . .
7. BOUNCE. . . . .
8. CAROUSE. . . . .
9. WAIST. . . . .
10. VARLET. . . . .
11. REVEL. . . . .
12. SHINGLE . . . .
13. LOUNGE . . . .
14. SHALLOW . . . .
15. STOOP. . . . .

Would You Get the Job?

A certain banker is said to test applicants for the position of teller by posing this problem: "I have here a check for $63. Give me that amount in six bills, please—but no one-dollar bills." If the applicant can't solve this in 30 seconds he doesn't get the job.

112

Word Gallery II 96

When Word Gallery (Test 56) appeared in The Reader's Digest, many readers accepted the challenge to create "word pictures" of their own. Here are some of the results:

WigWams

COUGʰ

bOsOm

fiRE!

swan

MEASLES

candles

INTOXᵇⁱᶜATED

SUNSᴱT

ALMOSʇ

EYE
DOC
TOR

T V

How Happy Are You? 97

ROBERT HARRINGTON

Most of us know when we're unhappy, and we're aware of fleeting joyous moments. But the question of just *how* happy one is can be difficult to answer. This quiz is based on traits found to be common among happy, well-adjusted people. Choose the response to each question closest to your own feeling or situation. If no response seems quite right you may check two, but no more.

1. Given your pick of the following jobs, which would you choose?

a. A difficult, challenging assignment. If you can bring this off, you'll be promoted to an executive job. b. A job you can excel in because it's ideally suited to your energies and talents. c. A fairly modest job that involves working closely with a very powerful, important person.

2. Do you enjoy doing favors?

a. Yes. I seldom refuse when asked. b. Yes, when it's convenient and will really *help* someone. c. Not really. But I oblige when I feel I owe it to the person or if there's some compelling reason.

3. Which description best fits your usual sleeping pattern?

a. Sound sleeper, little trouble falling asleep. b. Light sleeper, easily awakened. c. Sound sleeper, difficulty falling asleep.

4. Are there occasions when you need to be alone?

a. Absolutely. My most peaceful, creative moments are when I'm by myself. b. No. I love having people around. c. No. I don't mind being alone, but wouldn't say I have a need for it.

5. How important do you feel it is to keep your surroundings neat and orderly?

a. Very important. I can put up with sloppiness in others, but never in myself. b. Important. In fact, I wish I were more orderly. c. Fairly important. I'm rather neat and don't care much for mess or squalor. d. Unimportant. I'd rather be in a messy house where people are relaxed than in a tidy one where everybody's fussy and uptight.

6. Which of the following would you be *least* likely to want for a friend? The person who is ...

a. Snobbish and pretentious. b. A bully, cruel to those who can't fight back. c. Crude, pushy, ill-mannered.

7. In the past six months, how many times have you stayed home because of illness?

a. None. b. One. c. Two or more.

8. Something distressing has happened to a loved one—the death of someone close, perhaps. Your reaction?

a. I'd try to console him and cheer him up. b. I'd be as upset as he was—when he hurts, I hurt, too. c. I'd let him know I am sorry, but would continue to treat him the way I normally do.

9. How punctual are you?

a. Extremely punctual. I have an exact time sense. b. Quite *un*punctual. Even with an early start, I never get anywhere on time. c. It varies. I'm punctual for some things, late for others. d. Quite punctual. I usually arrive when I'm supposed to.

10. How long do you remain angry with someone who has been unfair to you?

a. A long time. I don't easily forgive bad treatment. b. I wouldn't get angry. Anger is the product of a troubled mind. c. Not long. I get angry, but seldom hold a grudge. d. I don't stay angry, but will usually avoid the person from then on.

11. You inherit several million dollars. How would you react?

a. I'd be delighted! b. I'd anticipate problems, but accept the money anyway. c. I'd be very worried about handling such a huge sum—it would mean starting a whole new life.

12. What would you find most appealing in a marriage partner?

a. Good-looking. b. Rich. c. Intelligent. d. Compatible. e. A terrific lover. f. Understanding.

13. Which statement best describes your social style?

a. I tend to keep to a small circle of close friends. b. I'm active

115

socially and know hundreds of people. c. I have a lot of friends but don't stay in touch with them. I usually associate with whoever comes to see me.

14. With which of the following would you agree?
   a. Time passes quickly, almost in a blur. b. Time moves slowly. c. Days are long, but weeks and months speed by. d. Days seem fast, weeks and months slow.

15. How do you feel about your present situation—personal qualities, friends and family, career, prospects for the future?
   a. Wonderful! And the future looks bright. b. Pretty good. My situation may not be marvelous, but it's okay, and improving steadily. c. Fair. But I'm striving for a much better future. d. My feelings vary. Sometimes I feel good about myself, sometimes not.

Punctuation Points 98

The following makes perfectly good sense once it's punctuated. Can you put the correct punctuation marks in the correct spots?

Smith where Jones had had had had had had had had had had had the examiner's approval

How Good a Witness Would You Be? 99

DR. GEORGE W. CRANE

Study this picture carefully for three minutes...then turn to the questions at the back of the book.

1. Place three glasses in a row, the middle one upside down. Pick up two at a time and turn them over. Make three of these moves—never turning the same two glasses in consecutive moves—and end with all upside down.

2. Grasp the stem of a wineglass in the second, third and little finger, and hold two lumps of sugar (or small dominoes), one on top of the other, in thumb and forefinger. Now put both lumps of sugar into the glass, one after the other, without using your other hand. (It's easy to toss the first lump and catch it in the glass, but much harder to get the second one in.)

3. Lay a calling card on top of a wineglass and place a nickel on the card. Now blow the nickel into the glass.

4. Hold a napkin at two corners and, without letting go, tie it into a knot.

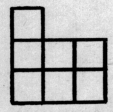

5. Arrange 20 toothpicks as shown above. Now remove three of the toothpicks and replace them so as to form a figure of only five squares—all the same size, and touching each other at some point.

Clarify Me This 101

MARTIN GARDNER

PROBLEM 1: Low Finance

"I seem to have overdrawn my account," said Mr. Green, "though I can't understand how. You see, I originally had $100 in the bank. Then I made six withdrawals. These withdrawals add up to $100 but, according to my records, there was only $99 in the bank to draw from. Let me show you the figures."

Mr. Green handed the bank president a sheet of paper:

WITHDRAWALS	AMOUNT LEFT
$50	$50
25	25
10	15
8	7
5	2
2	0
$100	$99

The bank president looked over the figures and smiled. "I appreciate your honesty, Mr. Green. But you owe us nothing."

Can you explain where the error lies?

PROBLEM 2: No Change

"Give me change for a dollar, please," said the customer.

"I'm sorry," said Miss Jones, the cashier, after searching through the cash register, "but I can't do it with the $1.15 in coins I have here."

"Can you change a half-dollar then?"

Miss Jones shook her head. In fact, she said, she couldn't even make change for a quarter, dime or nickel!

Assuming that none of the coins was a silver dollar, exactly what coins were in the cash register?

PROBLEM 3: The Three Neckties

Mr. Brown, Mr. Green and Mr. Black were lunching together. One wore a brown necktie, one a green tie, one a black. "Have you noticed," said the man with the green tie, "that although our ties have colors that match our names, not one of us has on a tie that matches his *own* name?"

"By golly, you're right!" exclaimed Mr. Brown.

What color tie was each man wearing?

-Graphy Is Groovy 102

GERARD MOSLER

If you were concerned with any of the 18 words in the left column, with which word in the right column would you be dealing? Match both columns, compare your results with the answers and get a graphic picture of your *graphy* knowledge.

1. Bibliography .... Handwriting
2. Cartography .... Codes
3. Anthography .... Books
4. Geography.. Mountains
5. Anemography... Spelling
6. Cryptography .... Printing
7. Ethnography... Earth
8. Hydrography .... Maps
9. Orography .... Heart
10. Topography..Stones
11. Choreography .... Flowers
12. Calligraphy .... X ray
13. Typography .... Localities
14. Phonography... Wind
15. Electrocardiography .... Sound
16. Radiography.. Water
17. Orthography... Dancing
18. Lithography.. People

Triple Meanings 103

BORIS RANDOLPH

Each triple definition below stands for a three-letter word. The answer to the first one is CUE. Can you find the others?

1. Acting signal, billiard stick, pigtail.

2. Pickpocket, downward slope, swim.

3. Tooth holder, rubber overshoe, chicle.

4. Son of Noah, kind of meat, bad actor.

5. Gratuity, extremity, advance information.

6. Line, boat ride, brawl.

7. Fate, great deal, movie studio.

8. Jail, quill, sty.

9. Dance, air trip, beer-flavoring plant.

10. Door opener, piano lever, Florida reef.

11. Greek god, metal dish, hard subsoil.

12. Harbor obstruction, drinking place, lever.

13. Attitude, atmosphere, song.

14. Joke, speech restrainer, fish.

15. Ball club, spree, winged mammal.

16. Haircut, pendulum weight, shilling.

17. Clothes fastener, bowling target, leg.

18. Radio chain, clear profit, snare.

19. Cravat, draw, railroad timber.

20. Pinch, cheese tang, small drink.

Buchwald's Quiz for Trouble-Prone Wives

104

ART BUCHWALD

In recent years, psychiatrists have discovered that every married couple has a "divorce potential." I'm happy to report to wives that there is now a test you can take to see how high *your* divorce potential is. Read the following descriptions of familiar situations. If any of the handlings of the situations fit your case, give yourself 10 points for each. Then check at the back of the book for your divorce potential rating.

1. It is after 1 a.m. Your husband has had a tiring day. You turn off the lights, and say:

   (a) "Why are the Chinese and the Russians arguing about communism?"
   (b) "My checkbook doesn't balance with my bank statement."
   (c) "Do you know what Betty Wheeler told me about Ann Sutherland?"
   (d) "I think I hear someone downstairs."

2. Your husband has just come home from work, and he is ready to make himself a dry martini when you say:

   (a) "I'm glad you're home. Someone has to pick up Jennifer at Ann Lindsay's house."
   (b) "Would you be a dear and carry Joel's bed down to the basement?"

(c) "I told a roofing salesman to drop by now to talk about a new roof."

(d) "I forgot to order gin."

3. Your husband is about to make a big deal at his office when you phone him and say:

(a) "The cleaner destroyed my new blue dress. I wish you would call him and give him heck."

(b) "Sears wants to know whether we want a blue mattress with a pink spread or a pink mattress with a blue spread."

(c) "What's the name of the man Jack Brody said will clean our chimney for practically nothing?"

(d) "I just wanted to hear your voice."

4. After a party you say to your husband:

(a) "Jerry Hammond says you're getting fat."

(b) "You didn't dance with me once this evening."

(c) "Who was that silly woman who kept giggling at all your old jokes?"

(d) "I don't know why you always want to go home just when I'm having fun."

5. Your husband asks where the car is. You reply:

(a) "Do you know the stop sign at Eighth and Main? Well, I didn't see it, and—"

(b) "The man at the repair shop said you have to put oil in the car to make it run."

(c) "I think it was towed away by the police when I parked in front of the supermarket."

(d) "I lent it to my brother while he is looking for a job."

6. Your husband is playing poker at your house with his cronies, and $100 is in the pot. You come in and say:

(a) "Would anybody like some chocolate fudge?"

(b) "My goodness, that's a lot of money!"

(c) "Don't pay any attention to me. I'll be quiet."

(d) "Who's winning?"

7. Your son has just flunked algebra, and you say to your husband:

   (a) "I told Joel you'd go see his teacher tomorrow morning."
   (b) "I told Joel you'd check his homework every night for a month."
   (c) "I told Joel you'd give him a licking when you came home."
   (d) "You talk to Joel. I can't."

8. Your husband is watching a pro-football game on TV. The score is 14-14, with two minutes to go. You enter the room and say:

   (a) "Which of these two dresses should I wear tonight?"
   (b) "The fuse in the kitchen just blew out."
   (c) "Would you make the salad before the guests come?"
   (d) "We're out of bread."

9. You have a fire in the house, and the second story is destroyed. Your husband says, "Well, at least we're insured." You reply:

   (a) "I forgot to pay the premium last month."
   You may forget the other three answers. That one will do it. You can get your divorce by mail.

Cut to Fit 105

SAMM S. BAKER

1. Charlie wouldn't receive his monthly allowance from home for another week yet. Meanwhile he had to pay his room and board or wind up on the street. When he explained matters to his landlady, she said she'd accept as payment a small gold chain he owned—a chain of seven precious links. To make sure he got proper meals all week long, Charlie offered to hand over one link of the chain each day. She agreed, but on condition that he cut *only one* link of the chain.

Charlie managed to solve the dilemma. His landlady received one additional link per day, for seven days. How was it done?

2. Can you cut a pie into *eight* pieces, by making only *three* cuts? You are not permitted to cut the pie in half and then put one half on top of the other before making the next cut. Nor are you allowed to cut it in layers.

Do You Have a Space-Age Mind? 106

GRACE MARMOR SPRUCH AND LARRY SPRUCH

In this era of space satellites, SALT talks and pocket computers, a certain level of scientific knowledge is essential to understanding many of today's basic issues. To test your level, try these 25 questions.

1. A kilometer is roughly (A) 1/10 of a mile (B) 5/8 of a mile (C) 8/5 of a mile (D) 2 miles.

2. Water freezes at (A) zero degrees Fahrenheit (B) 32 degrees Fahrenheit (C) 100 degrees Celsius (D) absolute zero.

3. A lunar eclipse can occur only when (A) the earth is between the sun and the moon (B) the moon is between the earth and the sun (C) the sun is between the moon and the earth (D) there is a new moon.

4. The conservation-of-energy principle refers to the fact that (A) it is essential not to waste natural gas and oil, for these are limited in supply (B) solar heating makes use of the sun's energy, which would otherwise be wasted (C) energy can be neither created nor destroyed (D) nuclear-power plants recycle spent fuel.

5. The splitting of an atomic nucleus into two large fragments and several smaller particles is known as (A) fusion (B) alpha decay (C) fission (D) thermonuclear energy.

6. Atoms are believed to be composed of (A) protons, neutrons and electrons (B) protons and electrons (C) positrons, neutrinos and electrons (D) protons and antiprotons.

7. The period of revolution of the moon about the earth is approximately (A) one hour (B) one day (C) one month (D) one year.

8. Identify the *non*-astronomical objects: (A) white spots and red midgets (B) white dwarfs and black holes (C) quasars and supernovae (D) neutron stars and galaxies.

9. A planet that is never visible to the naked eye is (A) Mercury (B) Venus (C) Mars (D) Neptune.

10. The chain reaction that forms the basis of the atomic bomb was first achieved by a group directed by (A) Albert Einstein (B) Niels Bohr (C) Edward Teller (D) Enrico Fermi.

11. The gravitational force between two spherical objects is known to be inversely proportional to the square of the distance between their centers. If that distance is made three times as large, the gravitational force will be (A) 3 times as small (B) 9 times as small (C) 2 times as small (D) 3 times as large.

12. Who did *not* make fundamental contributions to the science of electricity? (A) Charles Coulomb (B) Michael Faraday (C) Benjamin Franklin (D) Isaac Newton.

13. The Big Bang is related to (A) the hydrogen bomb (B) the maximum noise level in an amplifier (C) a theory of the origin of the universe (D) supersonic aircraft.

14. Nuclear physics does *not* deal with (A) alpha particles (B) beta rays (C) deuterons (D) deoxyribonucleic acid.

15. Radiocarbon dating is a technique by which (A) persons who might get along well together are identified by computer (B) the fading of carbon copies is used to discover the age of documents (C) the age of archeological artifacts is measured (D) the length of time that a patient has had cancer is determined.

16. A laser is *not* (A) a source of light that can be focused to a tiny area (B) a device conceived by Jules Verne for propelling a man to the moon (C) employed in some delicate eye operations (D) a device that was used to measure the distance to the moon.

17. Light (A) can travel in a vacuum (B) can travel at infinite speed (C) always travels in perfectly straight lines (D) cannot travel through solid objects.

129

18. A rocket moves because (A) its shape permits air to support it (B) it has exceptionally powerful propellers (C) it weighs less than the air it displaces (D) it pushes against its own exhaust.

19. The speed of sound (in air at sea level) is most nearly (A) 10 feet per second (B) 1000 feet per second (C) 10,000 feet per second (D) 186,000 miles per second.

20. Newton's three laws relate to (A) electricity (B) atomic physics (C) heat (D) motion.

21. A hologram is (A) a rapid means of communication (B) a slide that can be used to produce three-dimensional images (C) an atom smasher (D) a future mode of transportation.

22. The "Red Planet" is (A) Saturn (B) Venus (C) Sputnik (D) Mars.

23. A half-life is (A) a molecule that cannot be classed as definitely organic or definitely inorganic (B) half the average life expectancy of a group of people (C) the time for half a given amount of radioactive material to decay (D) the radiation dose that will be lethal to half the subjects in an experiment.

24. Give the proper order of the names Archimedes, Copernicus, Einstein and Galileo so that they correspond to these statements:
    —The first to view the moons of Jupiter through a telescope.
    —Showed the equivalence of mass and energy.
    —Stated that a floating body displaces a volume of water the weight of which equals the weight of the body.
    —Stated that the sun, not the earth, is at the center of the solar system.
    (A) Archimedes, Einstein, Galileo, Copernicus
    (B) Copernicus, Einstein, Archimedes, Galileo
    (C) Copernicus, Archimedes, Galileo, Einstein
    (D) Galileo, Einstein, Archimedes, Copernicus.

25. A topic *not* likely to arise in SALT talks is (A) NaCl (B) ICBM (C) MIRV (D) B-1.

The Colonel's 107
Quickfire Queries

One of the screwiest of all radio quiz programs was the one conducted by Colonel Lemuel Q. Stoopnagle who fired his daffy questions sometimes at guest celebrities, sometimes at members of the studio audience. Here are a dozen of his Quixie-Doodles. How would you fare if called upon to answer them in a hurry?

1. "Standing right where you are, on this hard wooden floor, how can you drop an egg three feet without breaking the shell?"

2. How can you throw a baseball with all your might, and have it stop and come right back to you...without hitting any wall, or obstruction of any kind?"

3. "How could you head your automobile south on an ordinary road, drive it for one mile, and without turning, find yourself a mile north of where you started?"

4. "Two fathers and two sons shot three rabbits. Yet each took home one rabbit. How was that possible?"

5. "If sneakers are used in tennis, cleats in football and spikes in baseball...in what sport are all-metal shoes used?"

6. "The attempt to commit a certain crime is punishable but the successful commission of the crime is never punishable. What crime is it?"

7. "After a man was blindfolded, someone hung up his hat. The man walked 100 yards, turned around and shot a bullet through his hat. How was that possible?"

8. "Suppose you wanted a log cut up. You called a farmer who said he would charge 50 cents to cut it into two pieces. But you wanted the log cut in four pieces. How much would the farmer charge?"

9. Of a person in the audience, Colonel Stoopnagle asked: "Can you seat yourself in any particular place in this theater where it would be impossible for me to do so?"

10. "In a regular nine-inning baseball game, if the home team makes two runs each inning and the visiting team makes one run each inning, what is the score at the end of the game?"

11. "In 1939 the Emperor of India visited this continent. What was his name?"

12. Asked of a person in the studio audience: "How can you put your left hand completely in your right-hand pants pocket . . . and your right hand completely in your left-hand pants pocket, both at the same time? Go ahead, try it."

Keep the Sounds in Line 108

MATT WEINSTOCK

Readers went nuts over this problem, posed by Roger V. Devlin of the Tulsa *Tribune:* What is the five-letter word whose pronunciation isn't changed by removal of four of the five letters?

A Curious Love Story 109

JOHN FISCHER

Recently some friends asked me to dinner to meet a visiting doctor from Ohio, a plump, comfortable man of about 60 who was in New York for a meeting of a psychiatric association. Afterward, over coffee, he said he would like to tell us a rather curious love story—to find out what we thought of it.

"A long time ago," he said, "there was only one bridge across the Ohio River between Cincinnati and Covington, Ky. Not far from the Cincinnati end of the bridge lived a lovely woman who was married to an elderly manufacturer of machine tools. Discovering after a few years that her husband was more interested in lathes than in her, she began to look about for solace.

"Eventually she found it, in the person of a handsome young sportsman who bred and trained race horses near Covington. She paid him frequent afternoon visits—always taking care to get home before her husband returned from the office.

"One spring afternoon, as she started her drive back to Cincinnati, she found that a flood was sweeping down the Ohio River. Foamy brown water was swirling over the floor planking of the bridge, the pilings were shaking as if they might give way at any moment.

"The only other way to cross the river was by ferry about a mile downstream. She hurried there and found, to her immense relief, that the boat was still running. When she looked in her purse for the fare, however, she saw that she had no money. Surely, though, the ferryman would trust her till tomorrow.

"He wouldn't. He explained that he would be glad to let her ride free if the decision were his own, but the ferry-owner had given him strict instructions not to grant credit to *anybody*. If he broke this rule, he would be fired. Sorry . . .

"The woman drove rapidly back to her lover's house and asked him for a dollar. To her astonishment, he too refused.

"'Don't you see,' he said, 'that if the question of money

133

should ever enter into our relationship—even a single dollar—everything would be changed? I love you far too much for that. You may think me ridiculously idealistic, but if you insist on demanding money from me I can never see you again.'

"Once more she drove toward the river, this time trembling with rage—a rage of fury at her lover and of fear for the wrath of her husband. She determined to force her way across the bridge in spite of hell and high water.

"She didn't make it, of course. Her body was never found."

The doctor paused for a sip of coffee, then asked, "Who do you think was responsible for the girl's death?"

Before you turn to the back of the book, answer the doctor's question yourself. You may find that the answer you give will reveal something about your own character—as it did to each one in the doctor's audience..

ANSWERS TO

TESTS & TEASERS

1. Who is the Engineer?

The brakeman, who lives halfway between Chicago and Detroit, also lives near Mr...., who earns three times as much as he does. Mr.... can't be Mr. Robinson, as Mr. Robinson lives in Detroit. He can't be Mr. Jones, as Mr. Jones' $20,000 a year isn't divisible by three. Therefore the brakeman's neighbor must be Mr. Smith. The passenger whose name is the same as the brakeman's lives in Chicago. He can't be Mr. Robinson, as Mr. Robinson lives in Detroit. He can't be Mr. Smith, as Mr. Smith is a neighbor of the brakeman, who lives halfway between Chicago and Detroit. Therefore he must be Mr. Jones. Therefore the brakeman's name is also Jones.

Smith beats the fireman at billiards, so the fireman must be Robinson. Therefore the engineer is Smith.

2. Twenty Questions

1. The Australian and New Zealand Army Corps.

2. Yes. From an airplane, with the plane's shadow directly in the center.

3. The ostrich.

4. Niagara Falls. The brink is receding about two and a half feet a year.

5. Yes. In maritime law, flotsam is the wreckage of a ship or its cargo found floating on the sea; jetsam is cargo cast overboard to lighten a vessel in distress, and usually refers to goods that sink.

6. He heard the last of the 12 strokes of midnight as he opened the door.

7. The only place he could be in such a position after walking south and west would be the North Pole. And the only bears there are polar—which are white.

8. Nothing. They were chosen as a distress signal in Morse code because of their simplicity—three dots, three dashes and three dots.

9. If a catcher drops the third strike and fails to throw the batter out at first, the man is safe.

10. By floating a small bit of butter on top of the cooking liquid.

11. Mexican jumping beans are small seeds occupied by the grubs of an insect which writhe and double up; this causes the bean to jump about.

12. Shivering increases muscular action, thereby heightening the heat of the body.

13. On the pads of his paws, on the nose and tongue.

14. Jim Corbett, one of the great boxers of all time.

15. Max Baer.

16. The hummingbird can.

17. Pale flashes of light seen infrequently over bogs and marshes at night, thought to be caused by the spontaneous combustion of methane and marsh gas.

18. President Harding in 1923.

19. An informal organization whose members all have used parachutes to save their lives. It is named in honor of the silkworms who supply raw materials for parachutes.

20. The "high seas" are those lying beyond the territorial bounds of any nation. The word is used as in "highways" and means the chief seas belonging to everybody.

3. Add a Little Something

• All the sentence needs is the letter *e:* Every evening Ernest earned eighteen cents exceedingly easily.

• A BIRD IN THE HAND IS WORTH TWO IN THE BUSH.
LOOK BEFORE YOU LEAP.
A STITCH IN TIME SAVES NINE.

4. Are You Creative?

TEST 1. 1. party 2. ball 3. cheese 4. cat 5. club 6. paper 7. finger 8. sugar 9. floor 10. green.
Creative individuals get 75 percent or more of these words right.

TESTS 2. Creative individuals usually check these responses: 1b, 2b, 3a, 4a, 5a, 6b, 7a, 8b, 9b, 10b, 11a, 12b.

TEST 3. Highly creative individuals tend to describe themselves by these adjectives: determined, sensitive, inventive, enthusiastic, absent-minded, independent, impulsive, unassuming, worrying, versatile, restless, reflective, moody.
Dr. Donald W. MacKinnon of the Institute of Personality

138

Assessment and Research has shown that the adjectives that the more creative individuals check as descriptive of themselves reveal that they have excellent self-images. Yet, paradoxically, they also chose the more unfavorable adjectives.

Dr. MacKinnon says: "One finds in these contrasting self-descriptions a hint of one of the most salient characteristics of the creative person, namely his courage. It is a personal courage of the mind, which often makes a person stand aside from society and in conflict with it. It is the courage to be oneself in the fullest sense, to grow into the person one is capable of becoming."

5. How Logical Are You?

1. Among the 97 percent of the women, if half wear two earrings and half none, this is the same as if each wore one. Assuming, then, that each of the 800 women is wearing one earring, there are 800 earrings.

2. Each barber must have cut the other's hair. The logician picked the barber who had given his rival the better haircut.

3. Adding the bellboy's $2 to the $12 that Smith paid produces a meaningless sum. Smith is out $12, of which the clerk has $10 and the bellboy $2. Smith got back $3, which accounts for the full amount of $15.

4. Zero. If three letters match the envelope, so will the fourth.

5. $13,212.

6. The customer had sugared his coffee before he found the dead fly.

7. The parrot was deaf.

8. Lower the barometer by a string from the roof to the street, pull it up, and measure the string. Or find the super and offer him the barometer if he will tell you the height.

6. Kangaroo Words

1. DEAD	8. IS	15. FACE
2. LIT	9. LIE	16. DEBATE
3. FICTION	10. APT	17. PANTS
4. SAVE	11. ROUND	18. RAIN
5. PART	12. SEE	19. SUPERIOR
6. TOMB	13. REVOLT	20. HOTEL
7. SATED	14. MART	

7. Can You Juggle Letters?

1.	TEAR	RIP	7. LIE	RECLINE
2.	DINED	ATE	8. SAVE	SALVAGE
3.	WHIRLED	SPUN	9. SHED	BARN
4.	GROOVE	RUT	10. SOUR	TART
5.	CUT	CARVE	11. FAT	PLUMP
6.	PET	CARESS	12. SLOPES	HILLS

8. CDB! (See the Bee)

I am an Indian. Oh, I see.
He is the one for you to see.
Ahchoo!
I am too old for you.
I am a human being. You are
    an animal.
The wine is excellent!
The elephant ate the hay.
I am seeing a gypsy.
Ham and eggs is healthy for you!

9. Quote or Misquote?

1. destruction (Proverbs 16:18) 2. paint (Shakespeare, *King John*) 3. learning (Pope, "An Essay on Criticism") 4. thought (Heywood, *Proverbs*) 5. savage breast (Congreve, *The Mourning Bride*) 6. of (Colton, *The Lacon*) 7. no fibs (Goldsmith, *She Stoops to Conquer*) 8. an ell (John Ray, *English Proverbs*) 9. very spice (Cowper, *The Task*) 10. The love of money (I Timothy 6:10) 11. nor any (Coleridge, *The Ancient Mariner*) 12. one life to lose (Nathan Hale)

10. One and Only

The word is "scythe."

11. Can Mice Sing?

1. Animals' eyes don't shine; that is, they don't give off light of their own. Yet, if we go into the woods at night and flash a light, we see eyeshine everywhere; little glitters of topaz to let us know that there is a spider hiding in this shrubbery, glints of green witchfire to betray the presence of a stealthy fox. But if we shine our light into human eyes, we rarely catch a glint. Why? Nocturnal animals' eyes shine for the same reason that roadside reflector buttons shine. Behind the retinas of these night explorers is what amounts to a cluster of mirrors. The faint moonlight or starlight in which they have to do their seeing is reflected by these mirrors and thereby multiplied.

2. By no means. They have complex eyes, fly with no indication of being dazzled even in the brightest sunshine.

3. They aren't. Bulls are color-blind.

4. All placental mammals are covered at birth by membrane; the slippery membrane around little porcupines renders them non-scratchy.

5. Every now and then a newspaper story tells how some astonished housewife has heard, or thinks she has heard, a mouse sing. No animalizer can attentively explore the night woods and fields for many years without finding that mice do have singing ability. The mouse song is a high, wiry, warbling little trill, somewhat like a canary's. Why don't we hear it oftener? Probably, though not certainly, because mouse music is mostly supersonic. Only occasionally does part of the song fall within our auditory range.

6. Well, not really, of course. What is true is that elephants have a good deal longer memories than most animals. They retain exceptionally the recollection of injuries. If an elephant has been done harm by a man, then sees the man again years later, the big beast may blaze up in a renewal of hatred.

7. Most killed animals are eaten at once by others. Animals that die of disease or accident may be taken, depending on the part of the world, by various big scavengers: vultures, jackals and so on. But an important part of the answer lies in the nocturnal activities of the extraordinary little creatures called sexton beetles. They can bury the body of a dead rabbit in a single night so that no trace remains.

8. No. Sea birds such as auks and murres make no nests, and neither do such common birds as nighthawks and whippoorwills. Killdeers and plovers merely scrape together a few pebbles before they lay their speckled eggs in a furrow of a plowed field. The cowbird lays her eggs in the nests of other birds, never builds one herself.

9. Keeping its toes curled firmly around a twig doesn't require a bird's conscious effort. The tendons that cause toe-curling pass around the

141

back of a bird's ankle joint. The instant the weight of a bird's body bends this joint, as the bird takes its perching position, the tendons pull the toes into a tight curve, clamping the perch firmly.

10. Perhaps no other single notion has been as responsible for the feeling that snakes are "nasty." It's altogether baseless. Snakes, one of the most fastidiously clean of all animals, are as dry and inoffensive to the touch as a smooth-bark tree.

11. The coil and strike are, of course, standard snake technique when there's time to arrange it; but a dangerous snake is dangerous in any position. Also, a rattler may strike without sounding its rattles at all.

12. The biggest vertical leap any fish can make is not much more than six feet. The "waterfalls" that fish ascend are mostly gradually slanted cascades and rapids, with plenty of whirlpools and back eddies. Salmon, reputed to jump up vertical waterfalls 20 feet high, really indulge in a vigorous jumping take-off followed by swimming. With the momentum of a jump for a starter (not straight, always at a broad angle), a salmon can flail and beat its way for a considerable distance.

13. Having no eyelids, fishes' eyes are perpetually open. But you and I, even with our eyes open, can turn off our consciousness of the seen, can elect to be blind. A tired fish similarly relaxes into unconsciousness. What little light of mind glimmers in that small brother-being of ours, down there on the gravelly bottom among the water weeds, dwindles even dimmer now, waning, drowsing and presently winking out. The lidless eyes are still open, but the fish is asleep.

14. In fact, yes. In spirit, no. A crocodile hasn't mind enough to enable it to indulge in an act as intricate as hypocrisy. It sheds tears whenever it opens its mouth to engulf a big victim, whenever its jaws are forced far apart, just as our own eyes water when we yawn.

15. A spider's web is spun of a dry and not-very-elastic sort of thread. As its final touch, the spider goes over it again, spinning a new kind of thread, gummy and sticky. It breaks its original guy spirals and replaces them with this. *This* is the spider web that catches prey, the viscid web-stuff that the spider carefully avoids after spinning. And the spider always leaves a "free zone" in this gummy network—a safe area where it can go scuttling with no danger of being entangled.

16. Yes, and so can many other big beasts, including elephants. When a horse stands stock-still and relaxes, its leg joints automatically lock to support it. It prefers to sleep that way. A recumbent horse sleeps only lightly and fitfully, and rarely stays lying down long. Its heavy weight, pressed against the ground, makes the horse sore and cramped, and makes its breathing laborious.

142

12. Are You a Genius?

(1) C. Omit the horizontal line in the asterisk, as it was omitted in the circle, (2) C. (3) E. The other words are nouns. (4) D and E. (5) 49; 9 is 3 squared, 16 is 4 squared. 25 is 5 squared, and so on. Also, 9+7=16, 16+9 =25, 25+11=36, and so on. (6) Earth. (7) 2. In each vertical and horizontal row, the second number is subtracted from the first. (8) Present. (9) B and C. All the others hold things together. (10) C. A whirlpool is part of the sea as a mountain is part of land. (11) 33. The difference between the numbers is progressively multiplied by 2. (12) B and D. (13) E. (14) 240. (24 × 10 and 12 × 20 both equal 240). (15) 768. It is not necessary to determine the values of A, B, C, D. Simply multiply × 32, (16) E. The others are all things that increase images or sounds. (17) A and D are synonyms. (18) D. The ball gets larger in each box, while the triangle remains the same size, and the ball and the triangle keep alternating positions. (19) A. Just the fact that Jim can't see a service station ahead doesn't mean there isn't one. (20) C. Positive and minus change positions; neutral stays in the same place.

Scoring

Give yourself one point for each correct answer. You receive an additional five points if you finished the test in less than 15 minutes, three points if you finished in less than 20 minutes, and two points if you finished in less than 25 minutes.

If you scored: 20-25 points: You are extremely intelligent—a perfect candidate for Mensa.

15-19 points: This should put you in the higher percentiles of the population—definitely a Mensa candidate.

10-14 points: Nothing to be ashamed of—a most respectable score. You should probably try the complete, standard Mensa test.

Fewer than 15 points: Forget about joining Mensa, but don't stew about it. You may just be having a bad day. Some of the most successful writers, businessmen, artists and other famous people don't have exceptionally high I.Q.s, either.

What's the verdict? If you think you may be Mensa material, or you'd like to receive membership information, write to Mensa, Dept. RD, 1701 W. Third St., Brooklyn, N.Y. 11223.

13. What's Missing?

1. The letters *Q* and *Z* are omitted.

2. The letter *e* is missing.

14. Oops!

Two errors are easy to find—*their* instead of *there*, and *errer* instead of *error*. The third error is the statement that there are three errors, when there are only two.

15. How Y's Are You?

1. ABYSS	11. YEARN
2. DRYING	12. PREPAY
3. YIELD	13. YEAST
4. YONDER	14. PLAYER
5. BUYER	15. SATYR
6. OYSTER	16. YEARLY
7. MAYBE	17. YODEL
8. STYMIE	18. DYNAMO
9. YACHT	19. ROYAL
10. HOYDEN	20. ASYLUM

16. Want to Bet?

1. Astonishingly, it's better than even money that two will have birth dates that coincide. How do you figure the odds? With any two people, the chances are 364 out of 365—express it as a fraction, a 364/365 probability—the dates won't match. The chance that a third person's birthday will miss both of theirs is 363/365; a fourth person's, 362/365; and so on. Multiply all these probabilities together, and by the time you have 23 people in the series, the chance of no matching birthdays falls slightly below 1/2.

When you have 30 people, the probability of a match is better than 7/10—or odds of 7 to 3 in favor. With 50 people, the chances are better than 97 out of 100! Test it next time you're in a crowd of 23 or more people. Or check 30 entries at random in Who's Who.

2. No. Believe it or not, the odds are 7 to 1 in the gambler's favor. It's the same principle as in Question 1; the same kind of probability calculation is involved.

3. There's a better than even chance of such a connection. ("It's a small world!") The average person is in direct touch with 500 people—each of whom is a link in many different chains of acquaintance spreading in all directions.

4. There is only one chance in four of an all-boy (B) or an all-girl (G) set. To work it out, note how many different, equally possible combinations there are: BBB, BBG, BGB, BGG, GBB, GBG, GGB, GGG. Of those eight sequences, only two—BBB and GGG—are all alike. So the probability is 2/8, or 1/4.

5. Most people guess a. But the answer is b. Listing all possible combinations—there are 16—we find in 6 of them a two-two split, in 8 a three-one split. So the probability is 8/16, or 1/2, that the sexes will split three and one.

6. It's exactly an even chance. No matter how many times a coin lands heads, the probability of heads (or tails) on the next flip remains 1/2. It is a fallacy to assume that one toss is related to, or in any way affects, future tosses.

17. Write Your Own Poem

> ...north & *south*...hoof & *mouth*
> curds & *whey*...Bob & *Ray*
> neck & *neck*...hunt & *peck*
> bill & *coo*...me & *you*
> push & *pull*...cock & *bull*
> pick & *choose*...P's & *Q's*
> ways & *means*...pork & *beans*
> love & *kisses*...Mr. & *Mrs.*
> heaven & *hell*...hail & *farewell.*

18. Are You a Scatterbrain?

The most logical interpretations of these proverbs are the "c" and "z" choices. If you scored seven out of ten you are normal in your perception, in your ability to interpret subtleties of speech and thought. Eight out of ten means you are sharper in comprehension than most. Nine out of ten indicates that you have an exceptional grasp of ideas. Ten out of ten? You're a philosopher!

Answers "a" and "y" are likely to appeal to the practical-minded person. If you checked one "a" or "y" there's a hint of a practical streak in your nature. Two such answers indicate a distinctly practical outlook, and three mean that practicality is your outstanding characteristic. More than three suggest that you carry practical-mindedness to an extreme which might mar your enjoyment of life.

Answers "b" and "w" are scatterbrain choices. They appeal to the person who cannot or will not concentrate and whose mind flits from one idea to another. One "b" or "w" answer does not mean much but if you picked two it hints that you have a frivolous streak. Three such answers would be a certain indication of scatterbrainedness. Four or more and you'd better think seriously of drastically disciplining your mind.

Answers "d" and "x" are the choices of a man or woman dominated by concepts of good and evil. Such a person is likely to judge others on the terms of his own rigid moral principles. On this test he can easily be attracted to an inaccurate answer merely because it seems like a noble sentiment.

If you picked one "d" or "x" you probably have a sound moral streak in your character. If you picked two you may be a little more righteous than necessary. Three "d" or "x" answers could be a warning to loosen up a little, lest you make your friends uncomfortable. Four or more such answers hint that you may need spiritual advice, for even righteousness can be carried to excess.

19. What Do You Know About the Sexes?

1. TRUE. Harvard University studies show that, when domestic differences arise, it's usually the spouse who does the most talking who gets his (or her) way.

2. FALSE. A two-year study conducted at Stanford University demonstrated that, other factors being equal, men are as much as 50 percent more proficient than women in solving complicated problems.

3. FALSE. Studies conducted by University of Southern California psychologists show that women are more subject to feeling depressed and "down in the dumps" than men.

4. TRUE. Authorities find that the average woman requires appreciably more sleep than the average man.

5. FALSE. Psychological studies show conclusively that, while minor emergencies tend to upset a woman more, in a real crisis she is likely to remain calmer than the average male.

6. FALSE. Leading university studies show that women are far more finicky about what they eat than men.

7. FALSE. Psychologists have found that women are more self-centered. They have fewer outside interests than men, are more preoccupied with personal concerns and problems.

8. FALSE. The American Institute of Family Relations, after careful evaluation of surveys, found: "Contrary to tradition it is not the wife's mother but the husband's mother who is the most frequent troublemaker."

9. TRUE. University of Minnesota investigators found that women discussed men far more often than men discussed women. Women talked about men more often than about any other subject—except other women. Men's conversations were most frequently devoted to business, money, other men—and then women.

10. FALSE. Veterans Administration psychologist Richard C. Cowden made an intensive study of married couples, subjected each husband and wife to tests designed to reveal their knowledge and understanding of the other's personality. Husbands had far better insight into their wives' character and were able to predict much more accurately how they would react under specific conditions.

11. TRUE. We can hear the women's protests: "Hah! You should see my husband when he has a cold!" Nevertheless, in a study of over 5000 men and women, sponsored by the Veterans Administration and Cornell University Medical College, it was found that women had a far greater tendency to exaggerate virtually all types of complaints and ailments.

12. FALSE. Psychological tests at De Paul University showed that though women were no less evasive than men, where outright lies were concerned, men led the field.

13. TRUE. Studies show that women tend to be attracted to men they can look up to intellectually. Men, on the other hand, tend to shy away from women who have more brains than they do. This doesn't mean that men are superior in general intelligence, but that men tend to "marry down," and women tend to "marry up."

14. FALSE. Studies conducted by sociologists at the University of Southern California show that men have much more difficulty in adjusting happily to a second marriage than women. Divorced men tend to become more "set in their ways," less willing to compromise, and to expect their next marriage partners to do most of the adjusting.

147

15. FALSE. Professor Leona E. Tyler, psychologist at the University of Oregon, evaluating the findings of leading scientific investigators, found the female begins to out-talk the male shortly after infancy. She talks more readily, longer and faster. But it is in verbal fluency, rather than in the grasp of verbal meanings, that females are superior.

16. FALSE. Studies show that men are more restless by temperament than women and much more easily bored by repetitive action. They lack women's capacity to adjust to monotonous conditions. Possibly one reason women are less bored by monotony is that they are more given to introspection and daydreaming.

17. TRUE. Numerous psychological studies on reaction time show that when a man's senses warn him of approaching danger, he reacts much faster than the average woman.

18. FALSE. Studies show that women not only have a greater capacity for happiness than men, but also for *unhappiness*. According to psychologist Lewis M. Terman at Stanford University, "Women experience the extremes of marital happiness and unhappiness more keenly than their husbands."

SCORING: Give youself ten points for each question answered correctly. When this quiz was pre-tested on men and women from all walks of life, *nobody* got all the answers right, and few answered even half correctly. So if you scored 50% or 60% correct, pat yourself on the back. A score of 70% is outstanding; 80 or 90% is terrific, and if you got 100%—we don't believe you!

20. Just Four Fun

$$3 = \frac{4+4+4}{4}$$

$$4 = 4(4-4)+4$$

$$5 = \frac{(4 \times 4)+4}{4}$$

$$6 = 4 + \frac{4+4}{4}$$

$$7 = \frac{44}{4} - 4$$

$$8 = 4+4+4-4$$

$$9 = 4+4+\frac{4}{4}$$

$$10 = \frac{44-4}{4}$$

$$11 = \frac{44}{\sqrt{4}+\sqrt{4}}$$

$$12 = \frac{44+4}{4}$$

$$13 = \frac{44}{4} + \sqrt{4}$$

$$14 = 4+4+4+\sqrt{4}$$

$$15 = \frac{44}{4} + 4$$

$$16 = 4+4+4+4$$

$$17 = (4 \times 4) + \frac{4}{4}$$

$$18 = (4 \times 4) + 4 - \sqrt{4}$$

21. Case of the Empty-Handed Musicians

2. Flute	5. Harp	8. Cymbals
3. Violin	6. Bassoon	9. Bass Viol
4. Harmonica	7. Trombone	10. Cello

22. Spellbinder

The correct spellings (source, *Webster's Third New International Dictionary*): 1. asinine 2. braggadocio 3. rarefy 4. liquefy 5. pavilion 6. vermilion 7. impostor 8. moccasin 9. accommodate 10. consensus 11. rococo 12. titillate 13. sacrilegious 14. mayonnaise 15. impresario 16. inoculate 17. supersede 18. obbligato 19. desiccate 20. resuscitate.

23. Danger: Loaded Questions

1. "FRUIT OF KNOWLEDGE." The Bible merely refers to the fruit of "the tree of the knowledge of good and evil." There is no evidence to suggest it was an apple.

2. CHARLES DUDLEY WARNER. This comment, generally attributed to Mark Twain, was actually made by Warner, a friend of Twain's.

3. BETWEEN THE YEARS 8 AND 4 B.C. The monk Dionysius, in the sixth century, first calculated Jesus' birth date, but later examination proved Dionysius wrong.

4. ABOUT SEVEN TIMES AS MUCH. At full moon the sun's rays shine straight down on the part we see so that none of the surface is in shadow. At half-moon the sun strikes obliquely on the part we see so that the tall mountains shadow much of the surface.

5. FRANKENSTEIN'S MONSTER. Frankenstein was the name of the scientist who created the monster.

6. NOBODY. There were never any snakes in Ireland.

7. DICTATOR. Caesar was never emperor—the empire was not formed until some years after his death. But he was made dictator for life.

8. ON BREEDS HILL. Bunker Hill is nearby.

9. THE 119TH. Nine planes and two dirigibles (one of which made two flights) preceded Lindbergh. He made the first nonstop *solo* flight.

24. Campfire Quiz

1. Three. Of any three socks taken out of the duffel bag, two must be the same color.

2. Plug, $2.25; paint 25 cents.

3. None, because the boat rises with the tide.

4. None.

5. He filled the three-ounce bottle and poured it into the five. Then he filled it again and poured it into the five until the five was full. That left one ounce in the three. Then he emptied the five back into the jug, and poured the one ounce that was in the three into the five. Then he filled the three and poured it into the five—making four ounces.

25. Are You a Word Detective?

1. STAR	5. LIVE	9. STAG
2. SLEEP	6. GUNS	10. BOG
3. PLUG	7. KEEP	11. WARD
4. STRAW	8. PART	12. DEVIL

26. Count 'Em Up

1. If there are eight men in a room and each shakes hands with each of the others once, there are but 28 handshakes—not 56, as many have guessed. Remember that when A shakes hands with B, B already has shaken hands with A and needn't do it again.

2. The bus stopped five times.

27. What Makes You Blush?

1. FALSE. People blush even when alone. "Solitary blushing" occurs when a person visualizes himself in a situation where he did blush or probably would blush.

2. TRUE. Blushing does not occur until a child has learned to be ashamed of certain feelings and to deny or conceal them to avoid disapproval. Usually, it comes after he is old enough to laugh at jokes.

3. FALSE. Men and women blush with equal ease.

4. FALSE. Blushing is common to all races. It has been observed in albinos, Negroes, Orientals, Polynesians and Brazilian aborigines, among others.

5. TRUE. Blushing occurs most frequently from puberty until the age of 30, then tends to diminish.

6. TRUE. In Victorian days, women were *expected* to blush as an indication of innocence. Today, women are no longer expected to blush at a *faux pas* or an off-color story—and generally they don't.

7. FALSE. A member of a group can be ashamed for what another member has done—and blush.

8. TRUE. If A sees B blush, he may assume that it is in response to the same sort of situation that would cause A to blush himself. He thereupon identifies with B—and blushes!

9. FALSE. Blushing may occur on the face, ears, neck and upper part of the chest. In certain tribes whose members habitually go naked, the blush may also be noticed on the abdomen and arms.

10. FALSE. Once a feeling of shame or embarrassment has been produced, there is no way in which a person can keep from blushing.

28. What's in Your Scrapbook?

1. SOCK	8. SPOOK	15. BROOK
2. PARK	9. ASP	16. BOOR
3. CROOK	10. COBRA	17. SCOOP
4. CRAB	11. BOA	18. ROOK
5. BOAR	12. COP	19. CAR
6. COOK	13. ROCK	20. CASK
7. OAK	14. SACK	

29. True or False?

These statements are not true. They are all false, because:

1. Cleopatra was the last of Egypt's Ptolemaic dynasty, which was actually Macedonian.

2. Frankenstein was the name of the medical student who created the monster in Mary Shelley's novel of 1818. The thing he made had no name.

3. The 21st century starts on January 1 in the year 2001. It takes a full 100 years to make a century, so 1 A.D. through 100 would be the 1st century: 101 through 200, the 2nd century; etc.

4. The North Star can guide you only so long as you're in the top half of the world. It can't be seen in the Southern Hemisphere.

5. Cream is lighter than milk. Why else would it rise to the top of the bottle?

6. There's a law against mutilating coins in such a way that they might be circulated afterward in damaged condition and so cheat the recipient. But drilling a hole in a coin, for example, and then using it as a piece of jewelry is not construed as defacement.

7. Others had flown nonstop across the Atlantic before Lindbergh. He was the first to fly solo.

8. The *Lusitania* made her first voyage in 1907. She had completed many trips before being torpedoed off the coast of Ireland.

9. The kilt was a form of male attire in ancient times and probably originated in the Mediterranean area. Both Roman and Assyrian soldiers wore them.

10. The first republican form of government appeared in Israel some 1400 years before Christ. The Greek republics came along many centuries later.

11. Porcupine quills fall out easily but only on contact. They can't be shot.

12. Being carbon, diamonds will burn in temperatures exceeding 1400 degrees Fahrenheit. This is hotter than most household blazes.

13. Technically, a pound of feathers is heavier than a pound of gold. Feathers are weighed by the avoirdupois system, in which a pound equals 7000 grains; gold by the troy system, in which a pound has 5760 grains.

30. How's Your Musical Geography?

1. Virginia ("Carry Me Back to Old Virginny"); 2. Tennessee ("Tennessee Waltz"); 3. Pennsylvania ("Pennsylvania Polka"); 4. Carolina—North or South ("Carolina in the Morning"); 5. California ("California, Here I Come"); 6. Oklahoma ("Oklahoma!"); 7. Alabama; 8. Texas ("The Yellow Rose of Texas"); 9. Georgia ("Sweet Georgia Brown"); 10. Pittsburgh ("Pittsburgh, Pennsylvania"); 11. New Orleans ("Way Down Yonder in New Orleans"); 12. San Francisco ("I Left My Heart in San Francisco"); 13. New York ("The Sidewalks of New York"); 14. Chattanooga ("Chattanoogie Shoeshine Boy"); 15. Dallas

("You're from Big D"); 16. St. Louis ("Meet Me in St. Louis, Louis"); 17. Kansas City ("Kansas City"); 18. Chicago ("Chicago"19. China ("On a Slow Boat to China"); 20. Glocca Morra ("How Are Things in Glocca Morra?"(: 21] Spain ("The Rain in Spain—falls mainly on the plain"); 22. Jericho ("Joshua Fit de Battle ob Jericho"); 23. Prague; 24. Paris ("I Love Paris"); 25. Scotland ("Loch Lomand"); 26. Avignon ("Sur le Pont d'Avignon"); 27. Bethlehem ("O Little Town of Bethlehem"); 28. Herald Square ("Give My Regards to Broadway"); 29. Old Smoky ("On Top of Old Smoky"); 30. Red River Valley ("Red River Valley"); 31. Dixie ("Dixie"); 32. Shenandoah ("Shenandoah"); 33. Grant Avenue ("Grant Avenue, San Francisco"); 34. Manhattan ("She's a Latin from Manhattan"); 35. 42nd Street ("42nd Street"); 36. America ("America the Beautiful").

31. You and the Weather

1. FALSE. From a physical standpoint you need it least then, when you are fortified by a backlog of spring energy. Chances are you most need your vacation in, say, January or February, after having worked at top speed since early fall.

2. TRUE. Medical studies show that babies conceived in the fall and winter tend to be heavier, those in October heaviest of all. It's because the mother's anabolism—building-up power—which influences the weight of her child is greater at this time. And these children tend to hold their relatively higher weights right on through their school years.

3. TRUE. Both people and animals get perverse, surly and unruly when a storm is brewing. Futhermore, our efficiency tends to be lowered when the barometer is falling, say the climatologists. Bus passengers forget a lot more packages at such times; traffic and industrial accidents soar. Dropping pressure has a bad effect even on our physical health, sometimes causing the critically ill to take a turn for the worse. Headaches and fainting spells increase, and surgeons often look for an outbreak of acute-appendicitis cases just before a storm.

4. FALSE. Just because most of us step livelier in winter to keep warm, we feel more efficient, but actually we aren't. Bodily efficiency drops as our energy and combustion levels rise; we waste more energy on any job in the cold.

5. FALSE. Despite the old adage that "a green winter makes a fat churchyard," studies in the northern United States show mildness brings a big drop in midwinter ailments. The winters that really fill the churchyard are those with many sudden changes.

153

6. FALSE. Girls in tropical climates on the average mature at 14 or 15, with fertility coming at about 18. The continuous devitalizing heat slows up both processes. But in stimulating temperate climates, girls mature about the end of their 12th year and reach fertility at about 15.

7. FALSE. You've had its symptoms—listlessness, low vitality and a desire for sleep. Physiologists will tell you spring fever is a very real upset. In adjusting itself to the sudden seasonal rise in temperature, your body must work extra hard to throw off the heat it needed in winter. The upshot is a drop in vitality.

8. TRUE. If you've kept notes on your spouse's temper—or yours—they'll confirm it. July is also tops for riots, criminal violence and hasty legislation. Oppressive heat and consequent loss of temper control are the causes.

9. TRUE. There's something about a damp or rainy spell which encourages it: no one knows just why. It's an old story to diaper services—they anticipate a booming business during bad weather, and an all-time high during the September equinox.

10. TRUE. One study, for instance, found that school discipline problems multiply about five times when the humidity breaks below 45 percent. Of course, this drop in humidity causes a general decline in self-control; adults get out of hand, too.

11. TRUE. And the reason given is this: The very same spring physical stimulus that makes for the health and fertility of normal people overstimulates the abnormal and weak-willed, causing them to go berserk.

12. TRUE. Except to midsummer heat, which they stand a lot better than the obese. But in other seasons the thin are more sensitive to weather than the fat. They store less calcium, vitamins, fats and water, and are not so well buffered to ward off the shocks of weather change.

13. FALSE. Of course a bright clear day inspires us, but apparently not to work. Studies show we accomplish most on dull days—no matter how we grumble and complain about them. If you want your husband to get something done around the house, ask him on a damp raw day.

14. TRUE. It's caused by the accompanying drop in temperature. You feel pepped up, work and play harder, and your concentration improves. If you do creative work this is the time to go all out, say the experts.

154

32. Vowel Play

1. Indivisibility.
2. Crypt, gypsy, lymph, myrrh, pygmy, sylph, tryst.
3. One thousand.

33. The Great Chain Puzzle

The answer is 45 cents. Take one of the groups of three links and break each one (cost, 15 cents). Then use each link to join two of the other groups (cost for three welding jobs at ten cents: 30 cents).

34. Quiz-Show Questions

1. Facing downstream, the left bank is to your left, right bank to your right.

2. (1) Cake-walk, (2) Big Apple, (3) Charleston.

3. Polydipsia.

4. False. The Ark of the Covenant was the sacred chest in the sanctuary of the temple into which Moses placed the tablets of stone containing the Ten Commandments.

5. Twelve: each Jack has two faces.

6. Yes. The House of Commons.

7. Embracery is the crime of trying to influence a jury or a judge corruptly.

8. "A rolling stone gathers no moss."

9. Because she would have been unable to tell of the dream if she had died of a heart attack in her sleep.

10. Milk.

11. Eight.

12. The flag should first be hoisted to the peak for an instant and then lowered to half-mast.

13. Descendant of the family.

14. Between Lakes Ontario and Erie.

15. Drum.

16. West side.

17. 88.

18. Ten: Mr. and Mrs. Smith, the seven daughters, and just one son as each sister had the same brother.

19. 200.

20. Two friends at the same time. Then you would have to buy only three admissions. If you took one friend twice, you would have to buy his ticket twice and your own twice as well.

21. Period, comma, colon, semicolon, interrogation mark, exclamation point, dash, hyphen, quotation marks, apostrophe, brackets, parentheses, braces, ellipses.

22. The end of the tongue.

23. One hour.

24. Shoes; socks; slippers; sneakers; sandals; snowshoes; skis; stockings; etc.

25. The strawberry.

26. Safe.

27. Zinc and copper.

28. A learned man.

29. Tea.

30. White with black stripes.

31. The match.

35. Sum Fun

Believe it or not, they both add up to the same—1,083,676,269.

36. Bewitched, Bothered or Befuddled?

BRONX VS. BROOKLYN
While the Brooklyn and Bronx trains arrive equally often—at ten-minute intervals—it happens that their schedules are such that the Bronx train always comes to this platform one minute after the Brooklyn train. Thus the Bronx train will be the first to arrive only if the young man happens to come to the subway platform during this one-minute interval. If he enters the station at any other time, the Brooklyn train will come first. Since the young man's arrival is random, the odds are nine to one for Brooklyn.

THE FORK IN THE ROAD
The logician points to one of the roads and says to the native, "If I were to ask if this road leads to the village, would you say 'yes'?" The native is forced to give the right answer, even if he is a liar! If the road does lead to the village, the liar would say, "No" to the *direct* question; but as the question is put, he lies and says he would reply, "Yes." Thus the logician can be certain that the road does lead to the village, whether the respondent is a truth-teller or a liar. On the other hand, if the road actually does not go to the village, the liar is forced in the same way to say, "No" to the question.

SCRAMBLED BOX TOPS
You can learn the contents of all three boxes by drawing just one marble. The key to the solution is your knowledge that the labels on all three boxes are incorrect. You must draw a marble from the box labeled "BW"—black-white. If the marble drawn is, say, black, you know then that the other marble in the box must be black also—otherwise the label would be correct. Since you have now identified the box containing two black marbles, you can at once tell the contents of the box marked "WW"—white-white. You know it cannot contain two white marbles, because its label has to be wrong; it cannot contain two black marbles, for you have identified that box; therefore it must contain one black marble and one white marble. The third box, of course, must then be the one holding two white marbles.

THE COUNTERFEIT COINS
The counterfeit stack can be identified by a single weighing of coins. Take one coin from the first stack, two from the second, three from the third, and so on to the entire ten coins of the tenth stack. Then weigh the whole sample collection on the scale. The excess weight of this collection, in number of grams, corresponds to the number of the counterfeit stack. For example, if the group of coins weighs seven grams more than it should, then the counterfeit stack must be No. 7, from which you took seven coins, each weighing one gram more than a genuine half-dollar.

157

37. What's Your Wife's Name?

Did it work?

38. What Do You Know About Eating?

1. TRUE. Poor breakfasts are likely to mar health, efficiency and marital bliss. Surveys show that breakfast-skippers (or skimpers) are more subject to deficiency diseases, make more mistakes at work and make poorer grades as students. Sociologists blame many family fights and even divorces on poor or insufficient breakfasts.

2. FALSE. Only psychologically. Calories are what add body heat. On a zero day the calories in ice cream will warm you as much as hot soup.

3. FALSE. It's good practice to cut down on indigestibles, but if you exercise a lot in summer and sit by the fireside all winter, you'll actually need more food in the hot months.

4. FALSE. Just about every food from pork chops to peppers has been considered aphrodisiac. Actually, the only connection between food and sex is that a well-balanced diet stimulates the body in every function. Malnutrition dulls every interest.

5. TRUE. Two extra snacks (not large meals) halfway between main meals—the routine of many school children, office workers and Britishers—provide quick-energy pickups, increase efficiency and make us less greedy at main meals.

6. TRUE. When you overeat one day you're hungrier the next. Huge meals stretch your stomach and throw your appetite out of proportion. Conversely, the less you eat the less you want—within limits, of course. After you become used to smaller intake you may wonder how you could have eaten so much previously.

7. FALSE. You'd have to climb 20 flights of stairs to lose the calories in one slice of bread, saw wood for 55 minutes to counteract one chocolate ice cream soda. And such strenuous exercise would only make you hungrier.

8. TRUE. Studies show tempers reach their peak just before breakfast, lunch and dinner. That's one reason not to ask a favor until after a meal—as every salesman knows well.

9. TRUE. A survey of 13- to 17-year-olds at St. Paul's School in Concord, N.H., showed they made good use of as many as 5000 calories

a day—three times their basal energy requirements. So don't worry if a teen-ager seems to overstuff—provided it's not all sweets.

10. FALSE. Fatigue gives you an abnormal appetite. But never eat heavily when you're overtired. Instead of the quick pickup you're after, the meal is likely to lie undigested and cause gastric complications.

11. TRUE. Fat people who claim they "eat like birds" aren't deceitful; either they eat little compared with what they'd like to eat or they fool themselves. In recent clinical tests a number of overweight people were put on a diet of what they *said* they ate. They proceeded to shed *five* pounds a day.

12. FALSE. A light snack or a cup of soup or milk before bedtime makes for a good rest. It draws blood into the digestive organs and away from the brain. Only if you overeat or choose heavy greasy foods are you in for trouble.

39. How Well-Lettered Are You?

1. Eye, ear, lip, arm, leg, rib, hip, toe, gum, jaw. (Few people get more than seven.)

2. J-A-C-K-P-O-T !

40. Break the Code

The solution is deceptively simple. The next two letters in the series are S, S. They stand for Six and Seven. And the first five letters stand for One, Two, Three, Four and Five.

41. What's Your Maturity Quotient?

For every *No* answer, credit yourself with the number of points indicated below, depending on the category. *Yes* answers score nothing. In Category A (immaturities with which most people can live without suffering serious consequences), every *No* answer is worth one point; in Category B (immaturities that are not too serious, though they do make life a little difficult), two points; in Category C (immaturities that definitely obstruct success, peace of mind, happiness), four points; in Category D (immaturities that are fairly serious but probably can be overcome), two points; in Category E (immaturities that are part of your natural life style—and therefore hard to overcome), one point.

Your grand total of points is your Maturity Quotient. A score of 75 or more is *super;* 65 is *excellent;* 55 is *good;* 45 is *fair;* 35 or below is *poor.* Keep in mind that only after the age of 60 are you likely to rate *super.* Age is not necessary for maturity, but the more years you live, the greater is your opportunity to develop your maturity score. If you score 75 in an earlier stage of life (and if it's an honest score based on genuine thought), then truly your maturity is extraordinary.

42. Arithmetics

1. 8 plus 8 plus 8 plus 88 plus 888 equals 1000.

2. The correct answer is 2100. If you said 3000, which is what most people come up with, you need practice.

3. If one and one half men can eat one and one half pies in one and one half minutes, twice as many men can eat twice as many pies in the same time. If three men can eat three pies in one and one half minutes, then one man can eat one pie in one and one half minutes. So in 30 minutes one man can eat 30 divided by one and one half, or 20 pies; and three men would be needed to eat 60 pies in 30 minutes.

4. You're on your own on this one. Many if not most good dictionaries will refresh your mind on how the Roman numeral system works.

5. Eighty minutes is, of course, exactly the same as one hour and 20 minutes.

43. Four-Minute Challenges

1. Using the thumb and index finger of each hand, carefully roll up the dollar bill from one end, permitting the roll to push the bottle slowly off the bill.

2. Move 7 to left of 2; 10 to right of 3; then 1 below and between 8 and 9.

3. Run around to the other side of the table and look!

4. Move the top card upward until the opened space forms a square.

5. With your left index finger press firmly on the nickel. With two right-hand fingers, slide the right-hand quarter to the right, then strike it firmly against the nickel. The left-hand quarter will spring aside. Move the right-hand quarter into the exposed space.

6. Remove any two inside matches that meet at a right angle. This leaves two squares, a small one inside the big one.

7. Don't. Just before tossing, he'll bend the match between thumb and forefinger.

160

44. What One Word?

1. Kind
2. Effects
3. Bow
4. Remains
5. Fence
6. Locks
7. Essay
8. Beam
9. Cross
10. Rear
11. Rash
12. Figure
13. Bluff
14. Bound
15. Bored
16. Grate
17. Gorge
18. Hose
19. Medium
20. Falls

45. The Triangle Game

Unless you are unusually perceptive (or unimaginative) you repeated or wrote "Paris in the Spring." But the triangle reads "Paris in *the the* Spring." Likewise the second triangle has two *a's* and the third two *the's*. An extensive test has shown that only one out of 40 persons can read these triangles correctly. Many fail even after several tries.

46. Try This for Fun

The most frequent answers are: Red, five, rose, apple.

47. "Information Please"

1. The campers at sea level. Water boils at 212 degrees at sea level, but the higher up you go the lower the boiling point. Therefore the water on the mountain, boiling at a lower temperature, will take longer to cook the eggs hard.

2. Bloomers were named after Mrs. Amelia Jenks Bloomer of New York, dress reformer of about 1850; sandwich, after the fourth Earl of Sandwich, who is credited with first making one to save time while playing cards; guillotine, after Dr. J. I. Guillotin, 1738-1814, who invented it; Vandyke, meaning a pointed beard, after the 17th-century Flemish artist; gerrymander, to divide an electoral area into districts so that one political party has an advantage in representation, after Elbridge Gerry, Governor of Massachusetts in 1812.

3. There are two participants on a tennis doubles team, four in polo, six in hockey, eight in crew, and ten in softball (with a roving fielder).

4. The equivalent of petrol is gasoline; multiple shops, chain stores; road diversion, detour; hire-purchase system, installment plan; butter muslin, cheese cloth. The British equivalent of garters is sock-suspenders; of run in a stocking, ladder; of bouncer, chucker-out; of "choo-choo," a "puff-puff."

5. The man in the moon could not hear his wife chatter because of absence of atmosphere. There must be some such substance as air to transmit sound waves.

6. Eamon De Valera. As a commander of the Irish Rebels in the Easter Rebellion, 1916, he was saved from execution because he was then an American citizen.

7. Terms common to music and baseball are: run; pitch; slide; score; tie; base (bass).

8. Arabs prefer white horses because they withstand the heat better. White absorbs and retains less heat than dark colors.

9. The Island of Reil is part of the brain.

10. Shakespeare never saw an actress. All roles were played by men and boys until many years after his death.

11. Mazuma—money; Mazola—cooking oil; Montezuma—Mexican emperor whom Cortez conquered in the 16th century; Zeugma—grammatical term from the Latin meaning "to join"; Sigma—Greek letter.

12. None. In total darkness it is impossible to see anything.

13. An airplane will fly backwards when the head wind is greater than its maximum air speed.

48. The Match Maneuver

Place three match heads together as shown, touching snugly. Then pile the remaining three matches on *top* of these with their heads similarly meshed. Thus, each of the six matches touches every other match firmly. Remember: in presenting the problem, no restriction was stated that the matches must all rest on a flat surface.

49. How Persuasive Are You?

Persuasiveness, of course, is never an exact science. People vary. The John Wolfe Institute of Houston, Texas, which has trained thousands of sales personnel in persuasive techniques, points out that occasionally the poorest techniques will work and the best will fail. Nevertheless, based on expert observation of ordinary situations like these, the Institute suggests the following as the answers that will *usually* produce the best results.

1. d) "My boss is coming to dinner next week..."
   When you show somebody how he may benefit by accepting your idea, he'll usually go along with you. And one of the most potent appeals is the prospect of monetary profit.

2. e) "I just heard you won the golf tournament..."
   A drunk is a hard man to reason with. But get him talking about something he wants to talk about, and he'll probably quiet down enough to tell you the whole story.

3. c) "I'm the one who goofed..."
   When you're wrong, your best chance is to admit it and give in gracefully.

4. b) "Don't you think it's better to take care of our needs..."
   A smart salesman always tailors his appeal to the individual he's trying to sell.

5. e) "My wallet is in my hip pocket."
   Be realistic. Sometimes the odds against you are too great. Whenever that happens, give up!

6. a) "I'm going to need your help..."
   To get cooperation from people, make them feel important.

7. c) "Let's make a deal..."
   Know when to compromise. You may have to lose a battle to win a war.

8. e) "You're the only one I'd trust..."
   There is virtually nothing that motivates people more than pride, triggered by an expression of confidence.

9. a) "I saw Dr. Mason..."
   This is one of the few times when "hard-sell" tactics work. If the doctor tells you to do something, you do it. Appeal to a man's natural instinct for self-preservation and you usually carry your point.

10. D) "I guess I was going pretty fast..."

Whenever you're confronted with the inevitable, especially a police officer, humility is the best policy.

If you've answered 8 to 10 questions correctly, you don't have to worry about your persuasive quotient. If you scored less than 8, it might be well to start analyzing your techniques.

50. Brain Teasers

1. The letter *n*.
2. BOOKKEEPER is one that should have come quickly to mind.

51. What Do You See?

It is nothing more than the word FLY, printed white on black instead of the more usual black on white.

52. Twist a Word

1. (a) DANGER
   (b) GARDEN
   (c) GANDER
   (d) RANGED
2. (a) TASSEL
   (b) STALES
   (c) STEALS
   (d) SLATES
3. (a) LAMENT
   (b) MANTEL
   (c) MANTLE
   (d) MENTAL
4. (a) SWORE
   (b) SOWER
   (c) OWERS
   (d) WORSE
5. (a) LAIR
   (b) RAIL
   (c) LIAR
   (d) ARIL

6. (a) ADDERS
   (b) READDS
   (c) DREADS
   (d) SADDER
7. (a) PASSER
   (b) SPARSE
   (c) SPEARS
   (d) SPARES
8. (a) EDAM
   (b) DAME
   (c) MEAD
   (d) MADE
9. (a) SOFTER
   (b) FOREST
   (c) FOSTER
   (d) FORTES
10. (a) LOSE
    (b) SOLE
    (c) SLOE
    (d) LEOS

53. Boil It Down

Remove ALL UNNECESSARY LETTERS and A LOGICAL SENTENCE will remain.

54. What's Your Energy I.Q.?

1. FALSE. Setting your air conditioner at 68 degrees would keep an Eskimo comfortable, but would hardly save energy.

2. FALSE. Normally a shower uses less water. But what's normal? A quick shower is one thing; a long soak is another.

3. FALSE. If you have air conditioning, *all* those measures will help keep the cold air in. If you don't, they'll help keep the hot air out. A 1/4-inch gap under an outside door lets as much air in or out as a 9-inch hole in the wall.

4. TRUE. It depends on where your thermostat is and the size of the fire. Fires need lots of air, and a roaring one may pull warm air out of the rest of the house to support combustion. If the thermostat is located in the room being warmed by the fire, the rest of the house will get cold.

5. FALSE. They could, of course, if you left them closed. But who would? The best guideline is: close draperies at night and on cold, gray days, and open them to let sunshine in. You may have to turn on a light on the bad days, but you're saving heat, and that's a good trade-off.

6. FALSE. Turn off incandescent lights but leave fluorescents burning if you plan to be back within an hour. It takes more energy to start a fluorescent bulb than to keep it burning that long.

7. FALSE. In winter, when your heating system is drying out the house, you can open the dishwasher early and let the dishes dry in the room air. Opening the dishwasher will also add some moisture to the air, like a humidifier, which is good for your furniture and good for you.

8. FALSE. Operate at full capacity whenever you can.

9. TRUE. Many foods can be cooked at a compromise setting. You could also bake several casseroles at one time and freeze those you're not using right away. Reheating takes a lot less energy than roasting or baking from scratch.

10. TRUE. And the fresh air and exercise may be good for you, too.

11. TRUE. "Instant-on" television sets have a device that keeps them "warmed up" all the time. The only way to prevent them from consuming electricity when they're not being operated is to pull the plug from the outlet.

12. TRUE. Each chunk of frozen food acts like a big ice cube and helps to keep the temperature down.

13. FALSE. Do them at night, when the peak industrial load has tapered off.

14. FALSE. Extra weight in the rear will give you better traction in snow, but otherwise is a drag that makes your car's engine work harder.

15. FALSE. If your air conditioner worked off your battery, you'd need a push before the week was out. Air conditioning turns your engine into a gas guzzler, so don't use it unless the outside temperature is unbearable.

16. FALSE. And that particularly applies to the winter drivers who start up the car and then wait not for the engine but for the interior of the car to warm up.

17. FALSE. Everything is true except the last item; there, you save gas by keeping the throttle steady and letting your speed drop as you go up hills.

18. TRUE. But knowing the right answer is only half the battle. Have you had your wheel alignment checked lately? Have you had your engine tuned in the last six months? And do you remember to check your tire pressure every two weeks?

19. FALSE. Radials look soft because of the way they're designed, but tests show that they give up to six percent better gas mileage than standard tires.

20. FALSE. Oil is a lubricant, not a wrench. If your car is so old or in such bad shape that it needs a really heavy oil, it probably shouldn't be on the road at all.

55. Bird Calls

1. f	6. j	11. d	16. c
2. k	7. h	12. o	17. l
3. m	8. a	13. g	18. r
4. p	9. q	14. n	19. e
5. i	10. s	15. t	20. b

56. Word Gallery

If you need further inspiration, look at Test 96.

57. Size Up Your Reasoning Power

Part One:
1—7, 13. 2—V, T. 3—G, M. 4—200. 5—L. 6—9, 15. 7—1, 3, 243. 8—11, 14. 9—23, 30. 10—B, W, V. 11—200.

Part Two:
Reading from left to right and from top to bottom:
A. 9-9-3, 3-9-9, 9-3-9
B. 9-9-9-7, 9-9-7-9, 7-9-9-9, 9-7-9-9
C. 9-8-9-8, 9-9-7-9, 8-9-9-8, 8-8-9-9

Part Three:
1-duck 2-gull 3-robin 4-crow 5-hen 6-pigeon 7-hawk 8-owl 9-parrot
10-sparrow 11-eagle 12-chicken 13-bluebird 14-blackbird 15-stork.

Credit yourself as follows:
2 points for each correct answer in Part One.
2 points for each correct answer in Part Two.
1 point for each correct answer in Part Three.

Total of all points is your score for these first three parts.
Superior	45–33
Good	32–27
Fair	26–21
Poor	20– 0
Your Score	————
Average Score	23

Part Four:
1. 1-F
2. 1-F, 2-T
3. 1-F, 2-T
4. 1-F, 2-F, 3-T
5. 1-F, 2-T, 3-F
6. 1-F, 2-F, 3-T
7. 1-F, 2-F, 3-T

Give yourself one point for each correct answer. A score of 15 is
excellent and ten is good.

58. Are You a Good Judge of Character?

Psychologists who use these questions to test candidates for personnel jobs say a score of seven correct answers means you're probably a pretty good judge of character. A score of six is passing. A score below five indicates you're substituting false stereotypes for direct observation. And what are the correct answers? According to scientists who have checked these beliefs against actual fact, all are false.

59. More Kangaroo Words

1. VACATE
2. URGE
3. SUE
4. LIES
5. RASCAL
6. IDLE
7. PRATE
8. DIVERS
9. RAGE
10. MATES
11. RAMBLE
12. PINNED
13. JOY
14. CAN
15. RULES
16. SPOTS
17. SLID
18. RIM
19. CUT
20. REST

60. Fascinating Fact Quiz

1. A steel ball bounces higher than a rubber ball.
2. Yes, in beer too—or in any carbonated drink.
3. A whip cracks because its tip moves faster than the speed of sound.
4. c) 100 times a second.
5. It proves the egg is hard-boiled. If uncooked or soft-boiled, a spinning egg will not rise up on end.
6. No. Celery is the dieter's friend.
7. c) The U.S. Postal Service guarantees no more than one-tenth calorie per stamp.
8. We swallow about a ton of food and drink per year.
9. A sneeze travels as fast as 100 m.p.h.
10. 50 miles. Human eyes are very sensitive.
11. Fingernails grow faster on the hand you favor.
12. It takes 43 muscles to frown.
13. A heart beats more than three billion times in 72 years.
14. No. Traditionally, a horse with all four hoofs on the ground means the rider died a natural death. Two hoofs in the air: he was killed on the battlefield. One hoof raised: he died from battle wounds.
15. d) more. There are at least 170,000,000,000,000,000,000,000,000,000 ways to play the first ten moves.
16. "Googol" is the word for the number 1 followed by 100 zeros.
17. Muhammad, the commonest name.
18. Tennessee.
19. It's the shortest one that includes all letters of the alphabet.

168

20. b) The caterpillar has about 2000 muscles.
21. c) 300 feet.
22. The sailfish—top speed 68 m.p.h.—is probably fastest.
23. c) 36,000 quills per porcupine.
24. Black on yellow—which explains the color of certain road signs, and school buses.
25. It happened on July 13 and 14 in 1977, during the great New York City blackout.
26. c) About 300 ad exposures per person per day.
27. Two cents an acre for Alaska.
28. True. In fact we spend $1.5 billion a year for sneakers.

61. How Do You Tell You're in Love?

Perhaps you thought *yes* answers revealed true love. Not so! It's the *no* reply that counts in each case except for Question 7. Here is why, according to the experts.

1. Real love does not happen all of a sudden. When people say, "We fell in love the moment we met," they actually mean that each corresponded to a certain ideal image held by the other. Most of us create these ideals in our minds whether we realize it or not. Thus, when we find someone who looks, acts and talks the way we imagined this special individual would, we are *attracted*—but that's all it is. Love can develop, but it takes time.

2. Jealousy is not a sign of true love. One of the greatest mistakes young people can make is to believe that the more violent the jealousy, the stronger the love. Some jealousy is normal between two people who care deeply about each other. But jealousy is really possessiveness, not love. Psychoanalyst Dr. Theodor Reik says that people who suffer acutely from jealousy often have an underlying sense of insecurity which leads to an overwhelming need to be loved. As a result, they can be extremely jealous even though they may not be in love at all.

3. Mooning, sighing and daydreaming are signs of infatuation, not love. Here's why: Real love is centered around the other person, with your whole behavior directed toward his or her welfare and happiness. Thus, a boy or girl in love can study and work comfortably, knowing he or she is thereby contributing to the other's happiness. Infatuation, on the other hand, is self-centered. The smitten one becomes absorbed in his own misery at being separated from the adored one or in daydreaming about her. He is in love with love, not a human being.

4. Love does not diminish when one is away from the loved one. If you love a person more when you are with him, chances are that your judgment is being influenced by the charm and excitement of his

presence. When he is not around to dazzle you, some doubts emerge as Dr. David R. Mace, executive director of the American Association of Marriage Counselors, put it: if you feel this way, indications are the love is superficial.

5. Love is not really blind to a beloved's faults. The person in love knows and understands the other's shortcomings but cares deeply nonetheless. The infatuated person has a tendency to regard the adored one as flawless.

6. An unhappy home life can trick you into thinking you're in love. The files of marriage counselors are filled with cases of young people who "fell in love" and married when all they really wanted was to escape from pressures they considered unbearable. For example, a young girl who is constantly battling with her parents sees her boy friend as the rescuing knight in shining armor who will "take her away from all this." She isn't in love—she just wants out.

7. Love cannot always perch on Cloud 9: it must be practical, too. Two of the most crucial elements in a marriage, experts point out, are money and children. Young people seriously in love must know each other's views on these topics. If a couple hasn't talked them out, chances are the romance hasn't reached the real love stage.

8. Love does not make lovers ill at ease. Dr. Mace declares that when the way you are impressing the other person is the dominant concern in a relationship, real love is still distant. When you know you are loved *for what you are*, you feel at ease in the other's presence.

9. Being companions in misery is not the same as being in love. Marriage partners should be able to share miseries, but such sharing is not in itself love. All too frequently, young people mix up the two and enter into marriage simply because each has discovered a fellow sufferer with whom to unite against an unfriendly background.

10. Love is a private bond between two people. Authorities agree it can't be real if one party permits intimate details of a relationship to be made public. It may be a bid for prestige in the group, but hardly love.

To score, give yourself ten points for each *no* answer, zero for each *yes* except in Question 7, where it's 10 for yes and zero for no. If you scored between 70 and 100, it looks like the real thing, while 50 to 60 indicates some uncertainty may exist. Get 40 or less? The romance may grow into love, but it's not there yet!

62. Not So Easy

Although the letter *e* is the most used letter in the English alphabet, here's a paragraph without a single *e*.

63. Word Play

Here is one solution for each question. (You may, however, have come up with other correct answers.)

1. Unite and untie.

2. Therein: the, there, he, her, here, ere, rein, in.

3. Hijinks.

4. Strength.

5. Startling, starting, staring, string, sting, sing, sin, in.

6. Queue.

7. AuTOMObile, oXYGen, joDHPurs, schiZOPhrenia, lun-cHEON or truncHEON, maRIJUana, saXOPhone, tOMAHAwk.

64. What One Word—II

1. HIDE	7. FILE	13. RIFLE
2. DRAW	8. MOUNT	14. PURSE
3. SULKY	9. RENT	15. PLAY
4. BAR	10. BOX	16. MEET
5. SACK	11. PLUCK	17. DISCHARGE
6. TRIP	12. HABIT	18. TUMBLERS

65. Try This Mystery Quiz

Maybe you've guessed by now what the quiz is all about. It's a tricky method of guessing how old you are by the names you give familiar objects—or in some cases, by finding out whether you remember the objects at all. If we're lucky, your score will add up to your age. But chances are we'll only come close. Here's how to tote up:

A. If you answered icebox, score 5; ice chest, score 8; refrigerator, 2.
B. Antimacassor or tidy, 8; doily, 5; no answer, 0.
C. Velocipede, 7; tricycle, 5; bike or three-wheeler, 2.
D. Wristwatch, 4; watch, 2.
E. Pompadour, 6; any other answer or no answer, 1.

F. Bongo drums, 2; any other answer or no answer, 5.

G. Plus-fours, 7; any other answer or no answer, 2.

H. Talking machine, 10; gramophone or graphophone, 9; victrola, 7; phonograph, 4; record-player or hi-fi, 2.

I. Rumble seat, 5; any other answer, 0.

J. Billy, 6; nightstick, 4; any other, 1.

K. Ice-cream freezer, 4; any other answer or no answer, 1.

L. Four-in-hand, 6; any other answer or no answer, 1.

Add up your score. Did we come close? Well, if we didn't, you're pretty spry for your age—or else wise beyond your years!

66. Numbers Game

This method was used by a number of the ancients, including the early Egyptians. It employs a principle of what we today call a binary number system (a base of 2 rather than 10), the same system used in computers. To understand it, one might begin by looking up "properties of numbers" and "binary number systems" in a mathematics textbook.

67. The World's Easiest Quiz

1. One hundred sixteen years, from 1337 to 1453.

2. Ecuador.

3. From sheep and horses.

4. A hard-wearing cotton fabric with a soft nap.

5. Sixteen. The one known as Louis XVII died in prison during the French Revolution and thus never reached the throne.

6. A large breed of dogs. The Latin name was *Insularia Canaria*— "Island of Dogs."

7. Albert. When he came to the throne in 1936 he respected the wish of Queen Victoria that no future king should be called Albert.

8. The distinctively colored parts are crimson.

9. Squirrel fur. (It may have got its name from a German inventor named Kemel.)

10. Thirty years, of course—1618 to 1648.

68. Man or Woman?

1. *Woman.* Says Dr. Helen Hall Jennings, clinical psychologist and professor of education: "Men won't split hairs, or be very conscious of details, where it doesn't matter. But women are apt to do so."

2. *Woman.* She thinks everybody wants to go, because she wants to go herself. According to a study at one university, confirmed by many others, a woman reacts to such questions subjectively—"how she feels"—while a man takes a broader, more objective view.

3. *Man.* Psychologist Richard C. Cowden tested a large number of married couples and discovered—to his amazement—that men had deeper insight into the minds of women than vice versa.

4. *Woman.* She is more eager to try new restaurants and new food items, according to nation-wide marketing studies and observations.

5. *Man.* Says Dr. Ernest Dichter, president of the Institute for Motivational Research: "A man is more curious than a woman, more likely to shop for new things, more impressed by ingenious packaging and new inventions."

6. *Woman.* Studies show that men generally decide on what they want *before* entering a store, while women make up their minds *after* entering.

7. *Man.* He is more apt to wait until the tank is nearly empty before gassing up, according to surveys by an oil company. A woman won't take that chance.

8. *Man.* "As a man, he's supposed to know his way around and he's reluctant to admit that he doesn't. A woman doesn't have her pride to consider, hence will ask directions," says Dr. Jennings.

9. *Woman.* Psychologists suggest that women are mainly concerned with *people*, while men's chief preoccupation is with *objects*. Therefore, women are inclined to leave car maintenance to their husbands.

10. *Man.* A car is a symbol of power to a man, explains the Institute for Motivational Research. A woman finds other ways to satisfy her ego.

11. *No difference!* Astonishingly, Dr. Jack Block of the University of California finds that men and women may feel emotion equally. The difference is in the way they show it. A woman weeps because it's expected of her; a man won't because it's "unmanly."

SCORING: Score 10 points for each correct answer, 20 for the bonus question. If you scored 30 or less, you're still a private in the Battle of the Sexes. 40 to 70? You're starting to catch on to the other sex. 80 or more? They can't fool you!

69. Are You a Shrewd Driver?

1. Don't panic; you can handle a blowout at any speed if you know how. *Don't brake;* that will only compound your steering difficulties. Grip the wheel hard, and *steer straight;* if you yank the car counter to its swerve, you might turn over. Give a little gas—on, off, on, off, lightly. This tends to restore steering control. When you've slowed down, lightly apply your brakes until you can safely turn off the road.

2. Don't slam on your brakes; with your front wheels turned so sharply, you could roll over. Instead, drift to the left side of the road (if no vehicle is coming) so you'll take the curve in a wider arc. At the same time, apply your footbrake in light spurts with your *left* foot while you maintain a light but constant pressure on the gas with your right (wheels under power hold a curve better).

3. Yank on the emergency brake with all your might. And shift to a lower gear if you have a stick shift—in order to take advantage of the braking effect of your engine. Pump your brake pedal up and down fast; this sometimes restores some braking power. As a last resort, if you're not slowing down, check your car by deliberately bumping it against roadside guardrails, hedges, fences, stone walls or even parked cars. You'll smash fenders and rip off paint, but eventually you'll stop—bruised maybe, but alive. Or, if absolutely necessary, "hit the ditch" at the likeliest soft spot.

4. Take your foot off the brake pedal. Then either throw yourself across the front seat or slump way down in the seat behind the steering wheel, so your head is supported by the backrest and won't be "whiplashed" when the truck strikes. Immediately after the impact, put your foot on the brake again if you can, so you won't roll into cross-traffic.

5. Slam on your footbrake and hold straight. Then let up a bit on the brake and swerve right, to pass *behind* the leftward-moving truck. *Don't swerve left*—that would put you in the truck's path. Don't hesitate to run off the road if you have to in order to miss the truck.

6. Don't slam on your brakes, for if you lock your wheels you'll lose all control. Instead, turn but don't jerk your steering wheel to the right, *into* the skid, and simultaneously let up on the gas pedal. Once steering has corrected the skid, apply your brakes gently, *in on-off touches*, to slow down.

7. Don't slam on your brakes or try to twist back onto the pavement immediately—that could turn you over. Hold hard onto the steering wheel, let up on the gas, steer the right wheels down the shoulder and gently "fan" your brakes on and off. When you've slowed down, remount the pavement.

174

8. Blast your horn; the driver may be asleep. Hit your brakes and head off the road to the right; you may change the head-on collision into a less dangerous "sideswipe." And keep going—to get out of the other car's reach. But if there is no time, in the crucial last second flip off your ignition to lessen chances of fire, and throw yourself onto the seat (or person) to the right, away from the steering wheel. Curl your legs tight to your torso and your arms to your chest.

70. Cash in Hand

1. One less groove—118—on a dime.

2. At least 20. On the face of the bill there's the word "Washington." But on the reverse side, in the ornamentation around the top of the building, there are tiny markings that reveal themselves, under a magnifying glass, as state names.

3. Only six times. But seven times if you put the bill in a vise for the last fold.

4. It means the bill replaces a mutilated one.

71. Nature-Fact or Nature-Fiction?

1. TRUE. Most savage animals are peculiarly infuriated by human terror—possibly, as some naturalists believe, because a frightened person gives off a "scent of fear."

2. TRUE. Only the female mosquito sucks blood; the male is content with nectar and other plant juices.

3. FALSE. Moss-growth depends chiefly on the exposure of the land and the direction of the prevailing winds.

4. FALSE. The chameleon's color-changes depend on temperature, emotion, health, and other factors unrelated to the chameleon's background.

5. TRUE. An adder, like all other snakes, is deaf.

6. FALSE. We're nearest the sun on January 2. We fail to get full benefit of its heat, however, because winter days are shorter, and the sun's rays are slanting.

7. FALSE. The beaver employs its tail as a rudder in swimming or as a prop when standing on its hind feet.

8. TRUE. Snakes are also immune to the venom of other snakes of their own species. The venom of a different species, however, can poison them.

9. TRUE. The horned toad's ejection of blood, which is intended to terrify enemies, is accompanied by a popping or clicking noise.

10. FALSE. The earthworm's "head" end will grow a new tail and survive, but the "tail" end will perish.

11. FALSE. Sharks often turn over in order to attack or grip their prey more advantageously in their undershot jaws, but they can bite effectively while in normal position.

12. FALSE. An elephant usually shows signs of senility at 50, and a centenarian is rare.

13. FALSE. Squirrels frequently forget where they hide part of their trove; their poor memory is an important factor in the propagation of forests.

72. Can You Fill In the O's?

1. VOODOO
2. SONOROUS
3. OFFSHOOT
4. OCTOROON
5. PROTOCOL
6. LOOKOUT
7. MONOTONOUS
8. STOREROOM
9. ORATORIO
10. CORROBORATOR
11. SOCIOLOGY
12. DOUBLOON
13. BOOHOO
14. ODOROUS
15. ROCOCO
16. FORENOON
17. OOLONG
18. FOOTLOOSE
19. ORTHODOX
20. HOMOLOGOUS

73. Alphabetease

Persevere ye perfect men, ever keep these precepts ten

74. Judge for Yourself!

SORE THUMB: Prisoner guilty. It makes no difference whether the wound was instantly mortal, or whether death resulted because Garland did not adopt the best mode of treatment. The real point is that the wound inflicted by the prisoner was the cause of death.

REGINA v. HOLLAND, 2 MOODY & ROBINSON 351.

THE CHERRY TREE: Sarah gets the cherries. The ownership of a tree is determined as the place where the trunk is located. Abner could have compelled Sarah to remove the overhanging limbs if he desired, since they interfered with the use of his land "upward to the sky." Not having done so, he cannot prevent her from taking her own property.

HOFFMAN v. ARMSTRONG, 46 BARB. (N.Y.) 337.

THE SPECIALIST: A substantial settlement for Anna Mohr. A patient's consent to an operation is a contract authorizing the surgeon to operate only to the extent of the consent given. Unless an emergency involving life and death is presented, the doctor is liable for an unauthorized incision. Correct diagnosis and skillful treatment is no defense.

MOHR v. WILLIAMS, 95 MINN. REP. 261.

THUMBED NOSES: Morris Garstenfeld was convicted. The court held that "the thumb to the nose and the fingers in the air" is "among boys a harmless vent for injured feelings . . . but when boys become men they should put away childish things. In the case at bar the circumstances . . . tend to show a design to engender strife."

PEO. EX REL. SHANNON v. GARSTENFELD, 92 MISC. 388.

"MARRY IN HASTE . . ." The husband wins. The law considers the parties bound immediately upon the solemnization of the civil ceremony. Parties may not make reservations to such a marriage contract. Once wed, the wife is bound to perform all the marital relationships. Failing to do so, she loses her marital right to support.

MIRIZIO v. MIRIZIO, 242 N.Y. 74.

KOSHER BACON: The complaint was held to be good. Even though a person means well and attempts to flatter another, if the words used injure his reputation the language is libelous.

BRAUN v. ARMOUR & CO., 228 APP. DIV. (N.Y.)
630, AFF'D. 254 N.Y. 514.

75. The Spy in the Rust-Colored Coat

The English spy sat with Mr. B on his right (line 5) and the window on his left (line 11). The spy in the olive coat is to the right of the German (line 7), so the German must be sitting in the other aisle seat, across from Mr. B. The Russian is in khaki (line 10), so he can't be the man in olive by the window, but must be Mr. B. By elimination, the man with the olive coat is American and the Englishman across from him is Mr. D (line 9). Mr. A is wearing a tan coat (line 6), so he must be the German. By elimination, Mr. C is the American spy—and it is the Englishman who has the rust-colored coat.

	Mr. C	Mr. A	
	American	German	
	Olive coat	Tan coat	
Window			Aisle
	Mr. D	Mr. B	
	English	Russian	
	Rust coat	Khaki coat	

Note that all relationships remain the same if you visualize windows on the right, aisle on the left—in effect, turning the above solution on its head.

76. How Much Do You Know About Men?

1. FALSE. Males come into the world with many more malformations and organic weaknesses. Their bodies are more likely to get out of order, and chemically don't function as efficiently. The male body is superior only in muscular development.

2. TRUE. Under average conditions, a man's body deteriorates more rapidly so that he is biologically older than a woman the same age. He is less resistant to most diseases, and with other hazards his remaining life span is shorter than the woman's.

3. FALSE. Males are better in mechanical, arithmetical and abstract reasoning problems; females, in language, rote memory, social and esthetic tests. Because of these differences, it is not possible to compare the intelligence of the sexes in equal terms.

4. TRUE. Psychological studies indicate less emotional balance in women.

5. FALSE. During the World War II bombing of London there were more cases of hysteria among male civilians, and the recovery of men under treatment was less rapid than among women.

6. TRUE. The male suicide rate is four times higher—in older age, almost eight times higher—probably because men are conditioned by society to take their failures more seriously or because illness hits them harder. If this fact and the fact that men are more hysterical doesn't seem to square with the statement that women are more emotional, remember the story of the reed that stood up in the storm when the oak cracked. Women, giving in more readily to emotion, yield to strain; men, more rigid, may crack under it.

7. TRUE. Color blindness is much more common in males and interest in color develops more rapidly in girls than boys.

8. TRUE. Women's bodies are better insulated with fat layers, and also function more efficiently in hormonal and chemical action.

9. FALSE. The most careful scientific tests fail to show any important differences in sensitivity to pain, or in the senses of smell, touch or taste.

10. TRUE. In aptitude tests, women are found to be superior where fine motions are required. The difference is revealed in early years, girls being able to button their clothes and to manipulate doorknobs before boys can.

11. FALSE. Both sexes inherit equally whatever hereditary factors there are for talent, but natural inhibiting influences (the female functions, childbearing, lesser drive) as well as social restraints prevent the expression of talent in women to the same degree as in men.

12. FALSE. Male infants are more restless in their sleep and don't sleep as long as girl infants, and this difference characterizes the sexes in maturity.

13. TRUE. Girls from earliest ages are more observant and conscious of people than boys. As they grow older women develop the power. This is helped along by the need of mothers to understand their children, sick people—and husbands.

77. Translation, Please

I ought naught to owe for I ate nothing.

78. Hit or Myth?

1. "c" is correct—though Nero set the fire himself and enjoyed watching the flames. He did not fiddle—the violin wasn't invented until 1500

years later. (He may have played the bagpipe, at which he was pretty good.)

2. "b" is correct. In years when the lemming population is high, lemmings migrate in search of food. Most of them drown while swimming out in search of another shore—if not killed first by larger predators.

3. "b" is the safe answer. Washington's father, Augustine, like other colonial plantation owners, probably experimented with plant breeding. It is at least possible that little George ruined a promising cherry tree, and confessed.

4. "b" is the wise answer. It is known that Lady Godiva's husband, "the Grand Old Earl of the Mercians," was beloved by his people, so it is difficult to imagine him levying a cruel tax. Some historians hold that an error of translation gave rise to the legend, and that "rode bare" should have been translated "rode bareback."

5. "c" is possible, but "b" is most likely correct. Reports that American survivors said it was "Nearer, My God, to Thee" are questionable. The English tune of the hymn (which the English musicians would have played) bears no resemblance to our own. Walter Lord, in researching his book *A Night to Remember*, interviewed all living survivors; none recalled "Nearer, My God, to Thee." Some claimed that the band was playing "light" music. But one crew member clearly recalled that, as the boat deck went under, the band was playing the Episcopal hymn "Autumn."

6. "b" is correct. According to Genesis 7:2, the Lord commanded Noah to take seven pairs of each "clean" animal and one pair of each "unclean" animal.

7. "c" is correct. According to the Library of Congress, Presidents Jackson, Buchanan, Lincoln, Garfield, Fillmore, Arthur and Pierce—seven in all—were born in log cabins.

8. "b" is correct. Recent excavations in England indicate that Arthur actually existed, though not necessarily as the romantic royal figure we have read about. But even the Swiss say that William Tell is a myth. And "Casey at the Bat" is pure fiction.

SCORING

Five correct answers means that you are a good guesser. Six correct: you are unusually levelheaded. Seven or eight correct: you are really *wise*. But whether or not your answers were correct, here are a few guesses about your personality that may surprise you:

If you answered five questions "a," you are a romantic. If you answered seven or more "a," you are an *incurable* romantic, always eager to believe anything that makes a good story.

If you answered five questions "b," you are a person who weighs things rather carefully. If you answered six or more "b," you are unusually levelheaded.

If you answered five questions "c," you tend to be a doubter. If you answered six or more "c," you are a real skeptic; you doubt everything on principle!

79. Questions for Young People, and for Parents

SCORING: Award five points for each correct answer, giving partial credit for part right. A rating of 80 to 100 shows that communications are excellent, while 55 to 75 means the lines are functioning fairly well. A score of 50 or below indicates a jam-up somewhere—so better start repairs, immediately. A hint: try listening a little more when the other generation is talking.

80. An "I.Q." Test

Liqueurs	Piquancy
Antiqued	Liquefy
Unique	Etiquette
Piqued	Communiqués
Clique	Semiquarterly
Piquet	Liquidating
Liquid	Oblique
Appliqué	Tourniquet

81. Pick the Champs

1. Sulphur-bottom whale; estimated at over 150 tons.

2. Sulphur-bottom whale.

3. Bison; over 2200 lbs.

4. Ostrich; over 300 lbs.

5. Reticulated python; over 30 feet.

6. Wandering albatross; as much as 11′ 6″.

7. Turtle; as long as 152 years.

8. Man; as long as 114 years, and perhaps even more.

9. Cheetah; over 70 m.p.h.

10. Moose; up to 1400 lbs.

11. Chimpanzee.

12. Vicuna; its hairs are only one half as coarse as the fibers of the finest sheep's wool.

13. Earthworm, according to agriculturists; it turns over the soil, thus increasing fertility of the land.

82. Lady in the Middle

1. Norma	3. Vera	5. Liz	7. Amy
2. Marie	4. Dora	6. Eve	8. Sue

83. Irish or English?

If the first man was English, he would have lied and answered, "I'm Irish." If he was Irish, he would have said so. In either case, the words blown away by the wind were "I'm Irish." So the second man is Irish, because he told the truth about what the first man said. Since the first two men are both Irish, the third is lying and therefore, obviously, is English.

84. Brain Busters

1. Usher: us, she, he, her

2. Sleeplessness

3. Add *e* to make "twelfth"

4. A *notable* doctor was *not able* to operate because he had *no table*.

5. Short

85. For the Parlor Psychologist

1. The age you choose generally represents the period when you either felt at the height of your powers or were happiest. Those who wish to return to infancy or early childhood suggest a lack of emotional maturity: they long for the period of no responsibility. Those who choose their present age are usually well-adjusted, successful people. Older men generally choose an age ten years or more younger. It's normal for a woman to want to stay 30 the rest of her life!

2. Those who would start out to make a new career are likely to be persons whose own efforts were responsible for their first success. If you would settle for a small routine job, you're sensible enough but don't have much spirit. If you would jump out the window, you're confessing to very few inner resources.

3. If the object is an article of clothing to cover your dishabille, you are cautious and conservative. If it's some sentimental keepsake, you are essentially a romantic. If you turn to a valuable possession, you are rather materialistic. If you grab your wallet or handbag containing your money, driver's license, and so on, you are practical.

4. If your answer is the place in which you have been living, your life probably has been satisfactory and full of interest. If you choose some remote place, you are somewhat of a dreamer. If you don't identify yourself with any place, you tend to be an unstable character with no strong attachment or loyalties.

5. If with your loved ones, you are of a deeply emotional nature. If alone, you are moody, discontented. Choosing one final fling indicates a fatalist, who would take whatever fate dishes out with equanimity. If you would keep the knowledge to yourself and spend the day as usual, you are a strong character.

6. Those who would turn to no one and get out of it themselves are supremely self-confident and tough. Those who would go to the family or close friends usually want to escape and be protected by passing on the responsibility. Those who would choose a lawyer or someone who might provide practical machinery for getting them out of their trouble are complete realists.

86. The World's Cussedest Quiz

1. Captain Kidd was hanged for murder. He hit one of his seamen over the head with a bucket and killed him. The charge of piracy was never proved.

2. The "Immaculate Conception" refers to the conception of Mary, not Jesus. The doctrine, made an article of faith by Pope Pius IX in 1854, holds that "the Blessed Virgin Mary, from the first instant of her conception, was by a most singular grace and privilege of Almighty God . . . preserved from all stain of Original Sin."

3. Waltz time.

4. The sun is nearest the earth in our winter season. It gives us less heat then because the earth's position is such that the rays come down slantwise, and a given amount of heat is distributed over much more surface than in summer.

5. This was not said by General Pershing. It was included in a speech at Lafayette's tomb, delivered by Charles E. Stanton, Chief Disbursing Officer of the American Expeditionary Force.

6. The comma should go after "Merry." "God rest ye merry" was a common greeting in early England.

7. A plant depends on the air for practically all its nourishment. It combines air with water by photosynthesis to manufacture its food. The soil provides only a trace of mineral foods.

8. Nineteen "witches" were hanged and one crushed with rocks. None was burned.

9. "Xmas" is a reverent form originating in the early Greek church. "Chi" (X) is the first letter of Christ's name in Greek, and it was frequently used as a holy symbol.

87. Could You Have Solved the Problem?

1. With the boy's finger pointed up, he wound a piece of string firmly around it just above the ring, pressing down the swollen flesh. After winding about a half inch toward the end of the finger, he started to unwind the string from the end nearest the ring, while another man pulled the ring up. As the winding and unwinding continued, the ring followed the string up and off the finger.

2. I moved slowly around the tree, staying just out of the dog's reach. He angrily followed me, winding his chain around the trunk until it was so short he couldn't possibly reach my car.

3. I simply clamped my hands tightly over his eyes. The pony, unable to see where he was going, came to a quick stop.

4. I placed my ear close to a bright light and the insect, attracted by the glow, immediately flew out.

88. Stung by a Spelling Bee

● He explains it:

phth	as in *phthisic*	— pronounced	T
olo	as in *colonel*	— pronounced	UR
gn	as in *gnat*	— pronounced	N
yrrh	as in *myrrh*	— pronounced	ER

● Potato. As this chap figures it: *gh* stands for *p* as in the last letters of *hiccough*...*ough* for *o* as in *dough*...*phth* for *t* as in *phthisic*...*eigh* for *a* as in *neighbor*...*tte* for *t* as in *cigarette*...and *eau* for *o* as in *beau*.

89. Look See

1. Each word contains three consecutive letters in their alphabetical order.

2. JUST ONE WORD.

90. Juggle Letters - II

1. SHED	BARN		11. ACHES	HURTS
2. SLAUGHTER	KILL		12. SPARSE	THIN
3. FRIGHT	SCARE		13. ALLY	FRIEND
4. SLIT	CUT		14. SAY	STATE
5. BOAT	SHIP		15. TEAR	REND
6. RING	PEAL		16. ASSERTS	AVERS
7. GO	LEAVE		17. BOOT	SHOE
8. CHOP	HEW		18. AS	LIKE
9. REGIMEN	DIET		19. RANTS	RAGES
10. PLANT	SOW		20. BARE	BALD

91. Mountains Out of Molehills

1. People who live in glass houses shouldn't throw stones. 2. The early bird catches the worm. 3. All that glitters is not gold. 4. Waste not, want not. 5. A fool and his money are soon parted. 6. It's an ill wind that blows nobody any good. 7. Look before you leap. 8. To err is human, to forgive divine.

92. How Masculine or Feminine Are You?

SCORE CHART
25-31. Very feminine. 32-36. Feminine. 37-43. Good masculine-feminine mixture. 44-47. Masculine. 48-50. Very masculine.

93. Pocket Calculations

1. You get there first—I miss the train. I'll try to arrive a short time before 4:05 by my watch. But 4:05 by my watch is in fact 4:15—past train time. You'll try to arrive a short time before 3:50 by your watch. But 3:50 by your watch is actually 3:45, well in advance of departure.

2. There are 10 birds and 20 animals. The problem may be expressed as an equation (with A for animals, B for birds): A + B = 30; 4A + 2B = 100.

94. Contract Word Game

(Dropping other letters in certain words may give you different results—but will your score be higher than the author's?)

		Pts.
1. THOROUGH: through, though, tough		3
2. MORON: Moon, moo		2
3. NATIVE: naive, nave, ave		3
4. BEREFT: beret, beet, bet, be		4
5. MANAGER: manage, mange, mane, man, an, a		6
6. CRACKLED: cracked, racked, raked, rake		4
7. BOUNCE: ounce, once, one, on		4
8. CAROUSE: arouse, rouse, ruse, use, us		5
9. WAIST: wait, wit, it, I		4
10. VARLET: valet, vale, ale		3
11. REVEL: reel, eel		2
12. SHINGLE: single, singe, sing, sin, in, I		6
13. LOUNGE: lunge, lung, lug		3
14. SHALLOW: hallow, hallo, hall, all		4
15. STOOP: stop, sop, so		3
		56

95. Would You Get the Job?

One $50 bill, one $5 bill, four $2 bills—total $63.

96. Word Gallery II

Did you come up with any brilliant creations of your own?

97. How Happy Are You?

Check your answers against the list below. Give yourself one point for each correct ("happy") answer.

1. b.	4. c	7. a or b	10. c	13. c
2. b	5. c	8. c	11. a	14. d
3. a	6. b	9. d	12. d	15. b

If you got two points or fewer, there isn't, unfortunately, much joy in your life. Four is better and six very good—you experience many happy moments. Seven points or more qualifies you as a happy person. Following is a description of each trait, along with the number or numbers of the questions where "right" answers suggest you possess these happy qualities.

The happy person likes to do useful, productive work, to use his abilities fully (1). He enjoys helping people, but is not self-sacrificing (2). At night, sleep researchers have found, he has little trouble falling asleep (3). He tends to be self-sufficient and can enjoy both solitude and company but is dependent on neither (4, 13). Generally, he's orderly and punctual (5, 9).

Though tolerant of people's minor flaws, the happy person dislikes cruelty and destructiveness (6). He is healthy (7), has no hang-ups about prosperity (11), and refuses to participate in other people's negative emotions (8)—*or* cling to his own (10). When choosing a mate, he will pick a congenial, compatible figure rather than someone romantic and glamorous (12). Like many busy, absorbed people, he feels days pass quickly, though in large units—weeks, months, years—time may seem endless (14). Finally, the happy person has a sense of progress, improvement, of getting somewhere (15).

98. Punctuation Points

Smith, where Jones had had "had had," had had "had." "Had had" had had the examiner's approval.

99. How Good a Witness Would You Be?

In the picture of the accident:

1. What was the name of the town?
2. What time of day was it?
3. What day of the week?
4. What season of the year?
5. Was the automobile a closed car?
6. What was its license number?
7. What direction was it going?
8. Did the driver have a hat or cap?
9. Was the boy bareheaded?
10. Which way was the bus going?
11. What was it number?
12. How many people were in it?
13. How many others saw the accident?
14. How many people in the picture?
15. On which street was the grocery?
16. Who owned it?
17. On what street was the hardware store?
18. What was its name?
19. What was in the window with the clock?
20. Was there a mailbox on the corner?
21. How many children were visible?
22. How many animals were shown?
23. Was the man in the window bare-headed?
24. Who had the right of way?
25. What was the price of bananas?

100. Parlor Puzzlers

1. Turn the second and third; then the first and third; and then the second and third.

2. Instead of tossing the second lump, simply let go of it and catch it by lowering the glass quickly.

3. Do not blow at the coin; blow into the mouth of the glass. The card's outer edge will tilt and the coin will slide into the glass.

4. Fold your arms before you grasp the diagonally opposite corners of the napkin; when you unfold your arms the napkin will have a knot in it.

5.

101. Clarify Me This

Solution 1: There is no reason whatever why Mr. Green's original deposit of $100 should equal the total of the amounts left after each withdrawal. It is just a coincidence that the total of the righthand column comes as close as it does to $100. This is easily seen by making charts to show a different series of withdrawals. Here are two possibilities:

WITHDRAWALS	AMOUNT LEFT
$ 99	$1
1	0
$100	1

Solution 2: If Miss Jones couldn't change a dollar, then there could not have been more than one half-dollar. If she couldn't change a half-dollar, then no more than a single quarter, and not more than four dimes. No change for a dime means no more than one nickel, and no change for a nickel means no more than four pennies. So the cash register could not have contained more than:

1 half-dollar	$ .50
1 quarter	.25
4 dimes	.40
1 nickel	.05
4 pennies	.04
	$1.24

A dollar's change can still be made with these coins. But since the register contained 9 cents less, eliminate the nickel and four pennies. The remaining coins—a half-dollar, a quarter and four dimes—are the $1.15 answer to the puzzle.

Solution 3: Mr. Brown couldn't be wearing a brown tie, for then it would correspond to his name. He couldn't be wearing a green tie because a tie of this color is on the man who asked him a question. Therefore Brown's tie must be black.
This leaves the green and brown ties to be worn respectively by Mr. Black and Mr. Green.

102. -Graphy Is Groovy

A score of 16 and over is excellent; 15—13 good; 12—11 fair; 10 average.

1. Bibliography .... Books
2. Cartography .... Maps
3. Anthography .... Flowers
4. Geography .... Earth
5. Anemography .... Wind
6. Cryptography .... Codes
7. Ethnography .... People
8. Hydrography .... Water
9. Orography .... Mountains
10. Topography .... Localities
11. Choreography .... Dancing
12. Calligraphy .... Handwriting
13. Typography .... Printing
14. Phonography .... Sound
15. Electrocardiography .... Heart

103. Triple Meanings

1. CUE	6. ROW	11. PAN	16. BOB
2. DIP	7. LOT	12. BAR	17. PIN
3. GUM	8. PEN	13. AIR	18. NET
4. HAM	9. HOP	14. GAG	19. TIE
5. TIP	10. KEY	15. BAT	20. NIP

104. Buchwald's Quiz for Trouble-Prone Wives

How high is *your* divorce potential? The author, an armchair psychologist and happily married humorist, says: "If you got up to 70 points, call your lawyer and ask him when the next plane leaves for Mexico."

105. Cut to Fit

1. Charlie solved the problem by cutting the third link—leaving him with sections of two, one and four links, as shown. *Monday:* He gave the landlady the single, separated link. *Tuesday:* Took back the one, gave her the two links. *Wednesday:* Gave her the single link. *Thursday:* Gave her the four links, took back the one and two. *Friday:* Gave her the single link. *Saturday:* Took back the one, gave her the two. *Sunday:* Gave her the remaining single link.

2. First make a circular cut within the pie, then two cuts across—as shown. Note that nothing was said about cutting equal pieces.

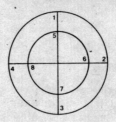

106. Do You Have a Space-Age Mind?

1. b	6. a	11. b	16. b	21. b
2. b	7. c	12. d	17. a	22. d
3. a	8. a	13. c	18. d	23. c
4. c	9. d	14. d	19. b	24. d
5. c	10. d	15. c	20. d	25. a

Scoring:

25-22 correct: exceptional; there may be a Nobel Prize in your future.

21-18 correct: excellent; with a little studying, you might qualify for a position in the space program.

17-14 correct: fair—but you could stand some homework.

13 or below: you won't qualify for that first trip to Mars.

107. The Colonel's Quickfire Queries

1. Drop the egg from a height of *four* feet. It will drop three feet without breaking. After that, what a mess!

2. A baseball will stop and come back to you if thrown straight up in the air.

3. By driving the car in reverse and going backward.

4. The two fathers and two sons were only three persons—a son, his father, and his father's father.

5. All-metal shoes are used in horse racing—the horse's shoes.

6. Suicide.

7. The hat was hung over the end of his gun.

8. $1.50. Because to cut the log in two only one cut is necessary; to cut the log into four pieces would take three cuts. At 50 cents per cut, that is $1.50.

9. The Colonel said: "The answer is, you could seat yourself in my lap. And certainly I could not sit in my own lap."

10. The answer is not 18 to 9, but 16 to 9 in favor of the home team. The home team never bats in the last half of the ninth inning when it is winning.

11. The name of the Emperor of India was George VI, who was also King of England.

12. The man said he could do it if he took his trousers off. The Colonel ruled quickly that the expected answer was that the stunt could be done if the pants were put on backward.

108. Keep the Sounds in Line

The word is Queue—pronounced simply "Q."

109. A Curious Love Story

The first of our group to answer was a New England woman who wore her hair combed in a tight bun. "What a silly question!" she said. "Obviously the girl had no one to blame but herself. She was morally responsible for her own acts, and she had to expect the consequences."

With some diffidence, our host disagreed. We all recognized, didn't we, that some women—present company excepted—are not fully responsible creatures? Some get emotional, even hysterical, on occasion. The ferryman, on the other hand, was presumably a levelheaded male, and there could be no excuse for his behavior. Instead of facing up to a decision in a moment of crisis, he had shoved the responsibility onto his absent employer. A clear case of moral cowardice...

Another guest argued that the ferryman had merely done his duty. He had made a promise to the boat-owner, and had stuck by it. But the girl's lover had behaved like a prig. In effect, he had sentenced her to death for the sake of his selfish, romantic notion about their affair. He seemed to be one of those doctrinaires who will sacrifice anything to their own fanatic concept of what is right.

"You're talking just like a man," our hostess said. "Any woman can see that it was all the husband's fault. If he hadn't been so awful, the poor girl never would have fallen in love with anybody else. And if he hadn't made her so scared of him, she wouldn't have tried to drive across that bridge. He was a hypocritical, authoritarian beast!"

A pretty blonde, curled up in a sofa corner, granted that husbands were often pretty beastly, all right. But couldn't the girl have phoned her husband that she would be staying overnight with an aunt in Covington? Or borrowed a dollar somewhere else? Or coaxed her lover out of his silly notions? And how old was that ferryman, anyhow? A girl can always find some way to wiggle out of almost any fix, so why did everybody keep talking about those tiresome moral decisions?

The argument went on until someone asked the doctor, "Well, what is the answer to your riddle?"

"I'm not sure," the doctor said. "Maybe everybody was partly to blame. That point doesn't interest me very much. You see, I often tell this story to patients at the beginning of a diagnosis. Their answers nearly always tell me something significant about their characters—as you have perhaps observed."